The Screenplay Sell

The Screenplay Sell

◆

What Every Writer Should Know

Alan Trustman

iUniverse, Inc.

New York Lincoln Shanghai

The Screenplay Sell
What Every Writer Should Know

iUniverse, Inc.

For information address:
iUniverse, Inc.
2021 Pine Lake Road, Suite 100
Lincoln, NE 68512
www.iuniverse.com

ISBN: 0-595-28084-6

Printed in the United States of America

Contents

CHAPTER 1   GENERAL PRINCIPLES. 1

CHAPTER 2   FOR WHOM THIS BELL TOLLS 5

CHAPTER 3   WHERE THE MONEY COMES
FROM AND WHERE IT GOES. 11

CHAPTER 4   WHY MOVIES COST SO MUCH. . . 17

CHAPTER 5   THE GREATEST SHIELD: THE
MOVIE DEVELOPMENT
BUSINESS 21

CHAPTER 6   WHO READS SCRIPTS? 27

CHAPTER 7   THE OXYMORON OF
COVERAGE. 31

CHAPTER 8   SACRIFICIAL LAMBS AND
"FRIENDSHIPS" 35

CHAPTER 9   THE ART OF THE PITCH 41

CHAPTER 10 PHONE ETIQUETTE, OR
RATHER THE ABSENCE OF IT 45

CHAPTER 11 MAILING AND THE
OVER-THE-TRANSOM SCRIPT . . . 51

CHAPTER 12 THE POWER OF AGENTS 57

CHAPTER 13 THE RESPONSES TO A
FORCED READ 69

CHAPTER 14 THE PACKAGE STALL 75

CHAPTER 15 REWRITER HEAVEN, WRITER
DEVELOPMENT HELL 79

CHAPTER 16 MAY HEAVEN PROTECT THE
WORKING WRITER 85

CHAPTER 17 THE PRELIMINARIES 91

CHAPTER 18 THE FIRST SOUL SEARCH 97

CHAPTER 19 THE SHORT HAPPY MOVIE
LIFE OF HARRISON STARR,
LINE PRODUCER 105

CHAPTER 20 THE SECOND SOUL SEARCH 119

CHAPTER 21 SOME WHO HAVE GONE WEST
AND MADE IT 125

CHAPTER 22 THE THIRD SOUL SEARCH 131

CHAPTER 23 PLAN A: THE GREEN-LIGHTER . . 135

CHAPTER 24 PLAN B: THE STAR ELEMENT . . . 143

CHAPTER 25 PLAN C: GET AN AGENT 149

CHAPTER 26 PLAN D: LURE A
PRODUCER IN 157

CHAPTER 27 PRODUCER ADVENTURES:
THEY CALL ME MR. TIBBS 161

CHAPTER 28 PRODUCER ADVENTURES:
LADY ICE 169

CHAPTER 29 PRODUCER ADVENTURES:
HIT! 179

CHAPTER 30 PRODUCER ADVENTURES:
CRIME AND PASSION 183

CHAPTER 31 PRODUCER ADVENTURES:
THE NEXT MAN 189

CHAPTER 32 PLAN E: GET THEE AN ANGEL . . 195

CHAPTER 33 PLAN F: THE INDEPENDENT
PRODUCER 201

I wrote THE THOMAS CROWN AFFAIR, BULLITT, five stinkers, ten uncrediteds and disappeared. Here's how and why and what you can learn from it.

1

GENERAL PRINCIPLES

It isn't what you know, it's whom you know. Nowhere is that more true than it is in the movie business.

To make the most money, you should involve yourself in as many movies as possible, and position yourself as far as possible from the actual making of the movies.

Movies get made when people agree to finance the productions.

Production financing agreements are based on packages. Packages consist of a bankable director, one or two bankable stars, and a concept, possibly a screenplay, but even if there is a screenplay the package will be based on the concept.

Production financing agreements and packages are both outgrowths of personal relationships.

The art form is the package, and the true geniuses of the movie business are the few producers who manage to package a succession of good movies year after year, and the extremely rare studio executives who preside over a prolonged run of consistent hits.

Nobody wants to read your screenplay.

Talent comes and talent goes and the industry continues to chew it up at an enormous rate because there is an inexhaustible supply of new, young, flavor of the month talented.

On the other hand, it is clearly in a sense a young person's business. Only the young have the energy, the relentless determination, the thickness of skin and the resilient hopefulness.

Hollywood is the city of dreamers,—and their dreams.

2

FOR WHOM THIS BELL TOLLS

All right. You have written a screenplay. That's great! Now what can you do with your screenplay?

Remember that everybody has ideas about movies. People know what they like and they know what they don't, which movies are entertaining and which ones are not, which ones they'll go to the theater for, which ones they'll rent, and which ones they won't see until they appear on television. People know the kinds of stories they like and which stars they like to watch. Some even know which directors make their kinds of movies.

Many, many people have ideas for movies. Some of those are good ideas. Many people fantasize about writing a screenplay, selling it for a huge amount of money, enjoying the success of the movie and living happily ever after. Some people even go so far as to write the screenplays, and some of those screenplays are pretty good.

Very few become movies.

Why not?

It is not that the writers don't try, and not that they don't try hard enough, but eventually they quit. How come? Because a disappointing series of rude rejections ultimately convinces them that it is just too difficult, too humiliating, too frustrating, too depressing and eventually they become discouraged by the apparent impossibility.

If you want to write a better screenplay, this book isn't going to help you much. Don't despair; there are lots of books, college and graduate courses, seminars and clinics out there teaching you how to write better screenplays. There are as many people willing to take your money to help you pursue that fantasy as there are waiting to profit from your desire to chase any other. A few of the books are very good, some of the courses truly helpful, and the seminars will at least introduce you to others who may be able to help, or at least commiserate with you. The same is true of the film festivals.

You can also go to film school and some of those are excellent, and not only those in Los Angeles. There are creative writing programs all across the country, and some of the lessons you would learn at those are applicable to the writing of screenplays.

This book is going to tell you how to sell your screenplay, something you're not going to find in most of those other books, or in the courses or seminars. If the people writing, teaching and leading those knew how to do that, they would be doing it, or representing you as an agent or manager and collecting fat commissions, or producing your screenplay movies.

If you think that having an excellent screenplay is enough, to get your movie sold and produced, you need to know a lot more about the business of making movies.

Is it really possible for an outsider to sell a screenplay to Hollywood and get his movie made?

Yes, would-be screenwriters, it certainly is, but only if you understand how the system works, and it works in some very, very strange ways. The gutters of Beverly Hills are filled with the emotional bones of talented young people who never did get it.

If you want to know what you have to know, this book is for you. Read it and weep not, but face the truth and you, too, can make it. And no, it is not all a crap shoot, and don't let anyone tell you that it is.

To get a feature film sold and made, you have to know as much about the business of Hollywood as you do about the art and craft of screenplay writing.

3

WHERE THE MONEY COMES FROM AND WHERE IT GOES

To begin with, the economics of the movie business are not at all what you probably think they are.

You assume they are making all that money because they are making such wonderful movies.

Nope. No way, that's not it at all. Theatrical box office continues to climb steadily year after year pretty much regardless of the quality of the movies being made, and it will continue to increase in the future as long as youth demographics and inflation remain favorable, and going to the movies continues to be a cool cheap date where you don't even have to talk for two hours.

Adults, young and older, may be getting tired of the endless stream of explosion movies with silly plots, and comic book characterizations devoid of personal relationships, but that has not been reflected in the ever-increasing box office. Not one bit.

Some years the movies do more business and in others, like this past year, the overall box office gross increase largely rode into the pockets of tinseltown on the back of ticket price inflation. Is a new generation of creative business genius multi-millionaires in part responsible for the steady gross box office progression? No, it is not, and there are no such geniuses with the exception of Harvey Weinstein. Anybody who can garner four of the five best picture Oscar nominations in a single year must be a genius at something, even if you are one of those who hate him. See Ken Auletta's recent NEW YORKER profile which is somewhat short of flattering.

Perhaps it has nothing to do with genius and there is a simple if not obvious reason: Harvey, who loves movies, makes movies, while all the others are making deals, except for John Calley, who makes a movie every once in a while when he gets bored with number-crunching.

Another common misconception is that the studios are making all that money because the not-so-wonderful movies they make are nevertheless making so much money, but no, that's not true either. In a sense, I suppose it is true, but the statement is quite misleading. For if you extrapolate two windfalls, neither of which the industry understood for several years after they were recognized on Wall Street, the industry has lost several billion dollars a year making new movies pretty much every year for many years. The two windfalls are videocassettes and foreign television.

The revenues from videocassettes have been huge, now there are equally profitable DVD's, and there will undoubtedly be in the future equally appealing and profitable new technologies. As for foreign television, if Mr. Karzai in Kabul decides to buy off a troublesome warlord by licensing him a new television channel, that channel will need immediate software, and the best and cheapest available software source is old Hollywood movies. Dubbing BULLITT in Farsi or whatever they speak in Afghanistan would cost maybe $25 and all the rest of the rental deal will be sheer profit to Warner Bros.

The two windfalls have together produced several hundred billion dollars of supplemental revenues, all of which the industry has distributed among the key players as if they have earned the money.

In a sense they have earned it, in the same way many other capitalist successes are achieved: by being in the right place at the right time.

Ironically proving the premise is the fact that the most money has been made by the people furthest removed from the making of movies: the investors who have controlled the movie companies. Some of them have achieved astonishingly poor results from the movies the companies they have controlled have made but they have walked off with billions in profits by doing nothing but riding the wave of the increasing value of company-owned old movie libraries.

The movie business has been very good to me. I love movies and I always have, and I love writing movies. Some day if I live long enough, I may even have another big movie. Meanwhile, I have been lavishly well paid for what I have done, and I have met some wonderful, talented people. I have made friends, some of them good friends, I have never been seriously hurt and, when I couldn't stand the heat, I promptly got out of the kitchen.

Some good people I like are not going to like what I say but there is no way I can tell you how to sell a screenplay and get it made without telling what I have learned along the way and explaining the industry as I think it really is.

So here is where I start to stray off the reservation.

What happens to all the money that is made, and we are talking about billions?

Paraphrasing Lord Acton, money corrupts, and lots of money, or the smell of it, corrupts absolutely. Since so much money has been made by the money men who have had nothing to do with the making of the movies, the executives running the studios have not unreasonably tended to be jealous, and have more or less consciously structured the industry so that they, and the A-list insiders, can get more and more of the pie, and shelter as much of it as possible from outsiders, including specifically the tens of thousands of eager young people who study film in the schools and arrive in Los Angeles in June of each year determined to make it big in the business.

4

WHY MOVIES COST SO MUCH

How have the studio executives gone about maximizing their share of all that money?

For one thing, they have tended to make more and more expensive movies, as the more a picture costs, and the more money that is spent on advertising and promotion, the more opportunities there are for the in-group to benefit, and the greater their control of the theatres, who want to book the latest and most heavily advertised pictures, and are afraid to book independently produced product with small advertising budgets as those pictures, with rare exceptions, cannot be expected to compete with studio movies costing today's average of $60 million to make and promoted with advertising blitzes costing today's average of $40 million. Moreover, although block booking, the practice of forcing theatres to take pictures they don't want in order to get the ones they do want, has been illegal for 60 years, any theatre chain that consistently shows small independent movies instead of the big budget studio movies, even the weakest of the studio movies, is taking the risk of not getting next year's studio hits.

Once upon a time, the studios owned their own theatres. Then that was declared illegal along with block booking, and for a while the theatres prospered, until they built so many screens that they became vulnerable to restricted production and national blitz release of insanely costly questionable value product with huge-budgeted advertising. In recent year, numerous theatre chains have gone bankrupt, and there is no need for the studios to own the theatres any more in order to control the theatres, which they do. Do not kid yourself. The major studios control the theatres. Just try to get good big city bookings for an independently produced picture.

Consequently the studios don't want to own the theatres any more. Indeed, why should they? Doing so would violate the first law of vertical integration as postulated by Michael Porter, Harvard Business School's strategy guru—never vertically integrate into a shitty business.

5

THE GREATEST SHIELD: THE MOVIE DEVELOPMENT BUSINESS

But the principal strategy for control by the in-group and exclusion of the kids and other outsiders has been the creation of a shield business, the movie development business. This has been a brilliantly successful strategy and it explains the structure and functioning of the industry, which is really two industries, one, the movie business and the other, its shield: the movie development business.

For every hundred people who will tell you they are in the movie business, 95 are not in the movie business at all. They are in the movie development business. They may say they are in the movie business, they may even think they are in the movie business, they certainly want to be in the movie business, and a few of them may someday be in the movie business, but in reality they are in the movie development business.

Some of them are writers and many of them are executives with impressive titles ending in "Development". They may be earning substantial six-figures year after year after year after year but they have never had a movie made and in all likelihood they never will. They have, however, been hypnotized by the bright lights, glamour and income and they will likely keep it up and keep hoping until their telephones one day stop ringing.

Do not ever ask them what movies they've actually made. In all probability, they haven't made any and, after all, you have gone to the trouble of setting up your meeting with them; that question will likely kill the meeting. If you want to know who you are talking to, before you go to the meeting get one of the industry credit books listing the movies on which people have worked. The list will very likely include a lot of titles you have never heard of. Only the pictures marked with asterisks have actually been produced and distributed. The rest of those listed are only development projects.

The industry spends an estimated half a billion dollars every year on the non-productive movie development business and it is cheap at the price. For no more than the cost of three big budget flops the inside group are able to keep control and all the rest of the money for themselves and keep the outsiders out of the business.

Which brings us to the studio structure.

In a perfect world, each studio would have a single executive who decides what movies to make, and a small support staff. The executive would succeed or fail according to the financial success of the movies he makes. Such a structure would, however, be anathema to the in-group since it would make the senior executive, as he should be, responsible for failure if he green-lighted the wrong movies.

Consequently the senior executives duck responsibility by hiring presidents of production and development, who in turn duck responsibility by hiring senior vice presidents and vice presidents of production and development. They in turn duck responsibility by hiring assistants, who in turn hire production executives, and they hire readers. To make certain no one at any level is ever to blame, we have at every major studio multiple lower and lower levels of executives.

That raises the obvious question: what is it that they do?

The Harvard Business School,—which I am now mentioning for the second time at the suggestion of my number one son, a brilliant technology guru executive and consultant, who went there and is a Baker Scholar graduate,—teaches that a good manager can manage anything. In practice, it is more true that a previously successful manager can get any job in management. Whether he can actually succeed in the new job without understanding either the new business or what the new company does is another matter entirely. My son, an alumnus of several New York stock exchange companies and several startups, tells me that the senior executives in many businesses in our country do next to nothing except enjoy their perks, talk on the telephone with each other, attend dinners and meetings, give each other prizes, options and increases in compensation, and make amateur decisions in areas where they have neither skill nor experience. That is a harsh criticism of American business generally and I am not competent to express an opinion about business generally, but I can say that that is a reasonably accurate description of the behavior of many executives in the movie business, and the movie development business.

They have nothing to do, and they don't do much of anything.

They talk on the telephone, hundreds of calls each day. They "take"—note the peculiar verb—breakfast, lunch, dinner and other meetings. They gossip, they spread rumors and they spend endless time playing vicious company politics. They are, in summary, incredibly busy—doing nothing. If you are granted access to their offices, you will see that they are littered with scripts, dozens, hundreds and sometimes thousands of scripts, which they are too busy ever to read. The piles of unread scripts are a necessary office decoration establishing visually that they do not read and could not possibly read their unread backlog; no one could conceivably read them all and they are much too busy. See?

They are of course too busy to return your phone calls or answer your letters, and the industry ethic does not require that they even try.

The level of competence and experience is best illustrated by the meeting of a well-known former studio head with all-time star director Fred Zinneman. The studio head graciously rose to greet the great man. "I'm honored to meet you, Mr. Zinneman, but I haven't read up on your career as I should. Tell me, what are your credits, sir?"

Fred Zinneman just looked at him. "You first," he said.

The studio head said nothing.

It was not a successful meeting.

Most studio heads do nothing and are therefore not in a position to say what they have done, unless they claim executive or associate producer credits on movies made in the studios they run, and some of them do claim such credits for exactly that reason.

What they should be doing is reading scripts.

6

WHO READS SCRIPTS?

They should be reading scripts, but they don't.

Why not? There are several reasons. In the first place, they will tell you they are too busy, and they are, doing nothing.

In the second place, they have embraced the widely-accepted Hollywood myth that nobody knows what the public will want, you can't even tell by screening the finished film, you can't tell from the rushes, and you certainly can't tell from the script, even if the movie were going to be shot from a script which was finished before principal photography, which is seldom the case, and that is another problem to which we will return.

"I don't read," a well-known studio head once told me proudly.

Back to the myth; it is not true. You can indeed tell from the finished film whether or not it is any good and whether or not it is likely to do much business, and there are people who can tell from the script because they can read the script and in their minds see the movie. You would think that someone who can read scripts has to have read the script before the studio committed $60 million to making the movie but that is generally not the case. The ability to read a script and imagine the movie is surprisingly rare in Hollywood and largely unknown among the studio executives who should be reading scripts, and who purport to read some scripts.

In sum, they can't read. Even more appalling, they know they can't read. The proof of that pudding is in the eating,—the tens of millions of dollars wasted, literally thrown away, every single year making movies that never should have been made because the scripts don't work, and don't even come close to working, and the chances of box office success if the script does not work are very very small, infinitesimal, although yes, it does happen.

The third reason they don't read scripts you have already guessed: if they read the scripts, they would be responsible for picking the scripts they want the studio to produce, and unable to pass the buck down the line to the junior executives.

They are too busy. They have convinced themselves that you can't tell from the script. They can't read and know it. They don't want to be responsible for selecting scripts. As a result, they don't want to read, any script, certainly not your script, and they won't, unless there is some unusually good reason.

The system is most awkward for the youngest vice presidents and production executives at the bottom of the food chain because the buck has passed down the line to them and you would think the buck stops there. It does not. To protect themselves, they have created the institution called coverage.

7

THE OXYMORON OF COVERAGE

Coverage is a three-page report written by a UCLA graduate student for $65 which summarizes the story and characters, suggests reasons for passing on the project, and concludes with something clever designed to cover the backside of the writer in the unlikely event someone else makes the movie and it is successful at the box office.

Coverage is almost always negative. It is intended to give the executive to whom it is furnished enough information so that he can pretend to have read the script and give intelligent reasons for rejecting it, with the polite suggestion that he would be interested in reading anything else the screenwriter might submit.

Coverage is often written by film school students or graduates who have not yet had any of their own scripts approved, but have figured out that if they want to make it in the business, it's more important to play the game than to evaluate fairly, recommend, or suggest, let alone edit other people's screenplays.

The executives often don't read the coverage anyway. They are quite likely to glance at it or skim it. They're too busy, doing, well, whatever they do, and besides, if they did read the coverage, they might be viewed as being responsible for agreeing with it.

In recent years, coverage has been refined even further. The first short paragraph on the first page is now a synopsis of the synopsis for executives who are too busy to read the synopsis.

The synopsis of the synopsis is still further refined to a one-sentence description on the cover page, a synopsis of the synopsis of the synopsis.

No, that is not a joke.

Many busy executives are likely to read only the cover page synopsis of the synopsis of the synopsis.

As for coverage almost always being negative, several years ago I was on an Austin Film Festival panel with three studio executives who had at one time been readers, and I asked each of them if he had ever written favorable coverage on a script. The answers were no, no and not really, whatever that meant. Point proven, I didn't ask her.

The certainty of negative coverage makes it highly dangerous to submit a script, any script. Although all the talent agencies as well as all the studios purport to hold their coverage confidential, negative coverage frequently manages to circulate throughout the town, effectively killing a script.

When coverage is circulated, the last page is taken off. That is the page where the $65 reader is allowed to express an opinion of the screenwriter as well as the script. For example, "Although this is a truly awful script, Mr. Goldman does write very well and we might wish to keep him in mind for future projects." The young reader may not have heard of Mr. Goldman before and might not have bothered to look up his credits, and the last page is consequently removed so the studio or agency will not be embarrassed.

8

SACRIFICIAL LAMBS AND "FRIENDSHIPS"

In fairness to the young executives, consider the position in which they find themselves. Average age, extraordinarily young, probably 27. Average pay, extraordinarily high, $200,000 to $600,000. Average job longevity, three years.

That's right, only three years. They have on the average three years to play the political game, affix themselves to a rising star, or a box office blockbuster, or a senior studio mentor, or they will be out. Gone. Period. They are in a real sense sacrificial lambs. If the studio makes stinkers, it will not be the senior executives who lose their jobs. Oh, no, it will all be the fault of the young production and development executives, who are young, and therefore supposed to know what the young movie-going public will like; that's their job, isn't it? A new crop will be hired and the old ones will be out on their ears.

It's a Ponzi scheme without the payoff. There is an inexhaustible supply of new eager beavers every year but instead of using their money and energy for the payoff of their predecessors, most of those will leave without it. Randomly, if that is a word, about one youngster in ten will be successful in any two year period, and the rest will be fired. Of every hundred who start, two years later, ten will remain. Two years after that it will be down to one, and he will be part of the industry. And probably a monster. He will have been trained to be a monster.

What can the young executives do, other than nothing, and other than read scripts, something which is dangerous, and which they know they can't do effectively, even if they wished to do it? They can play Dr. No for a while, turning down everything, secure in the knowledge that most scripts aren't very good, and most movies that are developed are never made.

Those negative recommendations will be correct, more than 95% of the time, but they really have to endorse something at least once or twice a year.

So instead they decide to make friends, and the way to make friends is to push packages.

The art form is the package, a clever producer is supposed to have said, and it is, if you are realistic. The package is not only the way that movies get made. It is the ticket from the movie development business into the real movie business.

What is a package? It is a project based on a short electrifying pitch, more later about pitches, a project to which an A-list director is willing to commit, necessarily involving at least one A-list male star, and one or more A- or B-list actresses, and possibly a screenplay by a current hot screenwriter, or at least the willingness of a current hot screenwriter to rewrite whatever screenplay may exist.

The young executive can safely give such a package an affirmative nudge, if not a push, because if the picture turns out to fail, as they usually do, he can defend his unfortunate recommendation by saying how could the studio say no to a package like that? Someone, somewhere, was bound to make that movie, and the studio could not afford to pass on it for fear that it might go somewhere else and there achieve box office success.

The young executive can also make a series of excited phonecalls to the offices of the producer, director or bankable star projecting his own personal enthusiasm for the project, and there is no better way to cultivate someone in Hollywood than to express enthusiasm for his project.

The only other projects the young sacrificial lamb might reasonably decide to push are those involving existing friends, assuming there is such a thing as friendship in Hollywood, or at least favorably-disposed acquaintances who are likely to employ or otherwise help the poor little lamb when he has lost his way and is out of a job next year.

My old friend, mentor and agent, the colorful and late-lamented-by-me David Begelman, used to say that there are no friendships in Hollywood, only affairs which last as long as the particular project is in play or the particular movie is in the theatres, unless the movie is doing big business at the box office in which event the affair may last until the next picture.

9

THE ART OF THE PITCH

Note that commitments are made and not infrequently projects are green-lighted on the basis of pitches, short electrifying pitches.

Pitches are normally presented at meetings, the industry being big on meetings, and such meetings are usually arranged by agents and so there will be no misunderstanding of the purpose of the meeting, they are called pitch meetings. A writer or producer is expected to prepare in advance of such a meeting a two- to five-minute project description, preferably cast in terms of major successful features of the previous five years.

It should be long enough so the meeting is not embarrassingly short, but short enough so the executive to whom the project is being pitched can remember it, and sufficiently exciting so there is a good chance that he will pitch it with the same degree of enthusiasm and in pretty much the same words both to his superiors and at the next department meeting, and so memorable that it will receive a unanimous endorsement and be pitched to the senior executive having go-power with the same electricity and again in the very same words.

Pitch meetings are to movies what sound bites are to news stories.

They are not unique to the movie development business. In other businesses, they are called "elevator pitches". They must be concise enough to be delivered and understood during an elevator ride, and sufficiently powerful to be remembered after the ride has ended. Hollywood doesn't have a lot of elevators, and most pitches are delivered in offices, so the term has been modified accordingly. Elevator pitches are in Hollywoodese just plain pitches.

There are people who are so good at them that they should be described as pitch artists. I once witnessed a breathtaking presentation by an extraordinary pitch artist, Jon Feltheimer, now Chief Executive Officer of Lion's Gate, of a project which I had agreed to write, and then found when I sat down to write the screenplay that I could remember vividly the light and warmth, but not a single word of what was said.

Do not ever submit a screenplay or submit a project until and unless you have prepared and memorized a powerful pitch, together with the appropriate enthusiastic facial expressions and voice modulations.

10

PHONE ETIQUETTE, OR RATHER THE ABSENCE OF IT

Maintaining this bizarre structure so that it has the appearance of functioning rationally and effectively as well as accomplishing its secret primary purposes, namely monopolizing wealth, protecting non-productive executives and excluding outsiders, has required the establishment of some highly unusual procedures, and general acceptance of such procedures as normal, rational and proper behavior.

Telephone calls are a major problem because one of the primary ways in which movie executives make themselves busy and chew up time is talking on the telephone. Accordingly, if you phone them, studio executives will neither take your call nor return it, unless you are on their A-list or B-list. They are too busy.

They receive and make an average of 70 phone calls a day. In fact, much of what they do to fill the hours is talk on the telephone. In the old days, they took A-list phone calls and interrupted other calls if need be. Today, A-list callers are usually called back the same day, unless the call recipient wishes to establish a senior position in the Hollywood pecking order, in which event he will call back very late in the day, or perhaps a day or two later. This absurd ethical lapse was the subject of a recent NEW YORK TIMES feature, and the article was perfectly accurate.

In the old days, B-list callers were called back by the end of the first day, or possibly on the following day, and C-list callers were called back late on the third day. Today, B-list callers are generally called back late on the third day and C-list calls, and outsider calls, are not returned. That is not considered rude;

callers are supposed to know the rules, and to know whether they are B- or C-list, or outsiders.

David Begelman taught me that in the old days, three days with no reply was a pass, you were supposed to know it, and it was rude to call again or otherwise prod. Today that sort of good manners, if that's what it was, is no longer prevalent, as calls may not be returned for weeks and months, if ever, even calls to people you know and consider friends.

Never phone on Monday. Studio executives are too busy and too harassed and hysterical flipping through their unreturned call list from the weeks before, and you are supposed to know it; if you phone then, you will make them angry. Never phone on Tuesday morning as most agencies and studios have large internal Tuesday morning meetings. Never phone late Thursday or on Friday because it is panic time again, and the unreturned call list is even longer. You may phone Tuesday after lunch through Thursday just before it.

Now suppose you are A-list or B-list, or a powerful agent or bankable producer, director or actor element has told the studio executive to take your call. You know your call will be returned, most probably in the next three days. It is your obligation to man your identified call-back phone line and keep it open from 10:00 am to 1:10 pm Los Angeles time and from 3:15 pm to 7:45 pm Los Angeles time for the next three days. He will only call you back once. If he gets a busy signal, a no-answer, an answering machine or voice mail, he may or may not leave a message and he will not phone again. He has no obligation to do so. You are the one who has been rude, and it is your ignorance or tough luck and he may not take your return call.

Once again, this is not a joke. When BULLITT was being packaged, McQueen, partner Bob Relyea, producer D'Antoni and star agent Kamen assembled a list of 100 possible directors, cut it to 25, and then to five, including my choice of Peter Yates, an unknown English director, whom I had selected for his brilliant car chase in ROBBERY, an unknown English picture which I liked and its studio and producer hated. The group then ranked the directors in order, one to five, and phoned the first name on the list. They got a busy signal. Oh, wasn't that too bad. They promptly phoned the second name on the list, and I was the only person present who considered what was happening at all peculiar.

The phone of the second man rang and rang. Eight rings, and they hung up, the call was over. And again, wasn't that too bad? I pointed out that it was 5:30 pm and maybe the man was home or on his way home from the office. That was a pity, who was next? Yates, I said, but it is 3:00 o'clock in the morning in England. Good, he'll be home, phone him. They did, and that's how Peter Yates made it in Hollywood when he got to direct BULLITT.

Managing and not answering phone calls is an art form. Assistants phone other people's assistants to wheedle out of them the times when their bosses go out to lunch, or go to see their analysts, or leave early to take a child to ballet class. You can then phone them when they are not in the office, without the necessity of talking to them, and you can accurately insist you returned the call. And that will be true. You did.

If you want to game the gamers, stay in and answer your phone at lunch time. The startled assistant who is calling will sputter that you should hold for Mr. whoever-it-is, and there will then be a silence, a long one, and then either an unexplained disconnect, or an "I'm sorry, he's taken another call, we'll get back to you shortly!"

Do not bother waiting.

At this point, the manner of presentation has to change as the industry is a strange and peculiar scene and specifics are the only way to explain the sort of personality you are likely to encounter and the remaining recommendations. You have just read a personal story and will now read more, getting to meet the people I met and learn what I slowly got to learn pretty much as it happened.

11

MAILING AND THE OVER-THE-TRANSOM SCRIPT

Every once in a great while, a script does come in "over the transom" and somebody reads it and likes it. Even then, the chances of something happening are not very great, but there are miracles in dreamland.

I was such a miracle.

After I wrote the first draft of THE THOMAS CROWN AFFAIR screenplay—which resembled no other screenplay anyone had ever seen since I had never seen a screenplay, did not know the form, and put on the page what the audience would see and hear—I optimistically mailed it to my favorite director, Alfred Hitchcock. A week or so later I got a phone call from a nice lady whose name I have long forgotten, one of my many indecencies since I owe her, and lady luck, my movie career.

"Who's this?" I said.

She gave me her name and said she was Alfred Hitchcock's secretary.

"Oh," I said, "that's wonderful. Does he like my script?"

"Of course not," she said. "He hasn't read it. What's more, he isn't going to read it."

"Why not?"

"Because he doesn't know you, and it doesn't come from an agent. Get yourself an agent."

"What's an agent?" I asked.

She laughed and told me.

I was suspicious. Why should I pay someone ten percent for remailing my script to someone else?

Because that's the way the business is run. "Look," she said, "I read it and I liked it."

"Even though it doesn't come from an agent?"

"You don't get it," she explained. "I'm an accident. The great man is on location and there's nothing at all going on in here so I read your Goddam screenplay. Get an agent, and that's all I have to say."

"Which is the biggest agency?" I asked.

She named the William Morris Agency.

"What's the name of the President?" I asked.

"Oh, come on," she said. "You've got to be kidding. His name is Abe Lastfogel but he isn't going to take your phone call. They must have hundreds of clients and they can't service most of those properly, they don't need new clients."

I thanked her, hung up and told my switchboard operator, Margaret, of sainted memory, and mind-blowing aggressiveness, to get Abe Lastfogel on the phone.

An hour and four furious phone arguments later, Margaret gave me the name of the head of the William Morris office in New York, which she had garnered from Abe Lastfogel's secretary who was desperate to get Margaret off the phone. Bernie Wilens. Margaret got him on the line.

"Who's this?" said Bernie.

"Never mind," I said. "I'm taking you to lunch at 21, tomorrow at exactly noontime."

"Do you have a name?" Bernie asked.

I told him.

We met for lunch the following day and that's how I got my first agent.

Notwithstanding my tale of good fortune, mail from outsiders is almost always brushed off with varying degrees of politeness and screenplays from outsiders that come in "over the transom" are invariably returned, unread, with the customary form note explaining that unsolicited screenplays are never accepted for reading unless they come from agents; please get an agent.

12

THE POWER OF AGENTS

Getting an agent is normally a catch-22. You can't get a screen-play read or pretend-read, covered, unless you have an agent, and normally you can't get an agent unless you have a deal on a screenplay and you ask the agent to represent you in the price negotiation. That is unquestionably the best way to get an agent.

Don't worry about the commission you will have to pay. The system is brilliantly structured to cover that concern. The agent will always negotiate a sufficiently higher price for your script to more than cover his commission, and the need for that will be recognized and accepted by all parties to the transaction.

What else can you expect from an agent?

Not much. An agent can open doors for you and set up pitch meetings, but most pitch meetings are useless exercises in frus-tration. Robert Altman's masterpiece, THE PLAYER—an hilarious send-up of the industry or rather, what it might be like, if there were no agents, and believe it or not, in the movie, there are no agents—has a sequence in which successful screen-writers mock-pitch projects in scenes that are screamingly funny unless you understand that the ridiculous dialogue you are enjoying is exactly the sort of thing that happens at most Los Angeles pitch meetings.

Furthermore, screenwriters beware: a series of fruitless agent-arranged pitch meetings may be a stall, preliminary to a brush-off, by your agent. A pitch meeting is highly likely to be a com-plete waste of time by all parties,—unless there is some major element involved whom the agency also represents, and if that is the case, you will know it. Always remember that agencies are looking to represent packages, and the more elements they represent in a project, the more serious, energetic and determined salesmen they are likely to be. A naked script without an attached element is unlikely to be taken seriously, and a naked screenwriter with a series of pitches is a pathetic innocent who does not understand that neither the agent nor the pitchee is taking the meeting seriously and the pitchee is merely accommodating the agent by wasting time on the meeting.

There are rare, unusual agents, who do more. Bernie Wilens had no idea what to do with me and correctly sensed that I was likely to be difficult, so he turned me over to a new hire, John Flaxman, an eager beaver and a genius agent. Flaxman worked on the script with me for months, draft after draft after draft, without making the slightest effort to change my novel, non-screenplay format, which he saw as a helpful marketing ploy if and when we got to that stage. He also cultivated my addiction to our constant phone and personal conversations. After a couple of months of this, I became edgy if two of three days went by without a phone call from Flaxman.

One memorable morning he phoned after reviewing my latest redraft and instructed me curtly that I was not to take any phone calls from anyone I didn't know in New York or Los Angeles. Why? It was too complicated to explain. Just don't pick up the telephone.

What he was doing without telling me was absolutely brilliant agenting. Norman Jewison was on his way back from Moscow to Los Angeles where the Russians had crushed him by not finding THE RUSSIANS ARE COMING at all amusing. I thought the movie was very funny but apparently it did not appeal to the Russians. Flaxman had my script delivered to Jewison at JFK, when he changed planes for Los Angeles, and told him he had exactly ten minutes from the landing in Los Angeles to phone in and say yes or no. Jewison said yes. Flaxman gave him 24 hours to get the project blessed by producer Walter Mirisch and studio United Artists, and Jewison delivered. A star was born. Me. An asshole with an ego and no people skills, but apparently with some talent.

Flaxman later set up BULLITT for me, producer Phil D'Antoni, and producer-actor Steve McQueen, a second home run for the agency who once again represented not only me but a number of the other elements in the picture. Following his BULLITT triumph, however, Abe Lastfogel ordered Flaxman to move from New York to Los Angeles and told him he had to relocate at once to have any sort of future with William Morris. Being a genius, Flaxman promptly quit. I have never met anyone like him. As an agent, he was perfect.

Almost.

Flaxman had a second promising client, a Yale professor of Greek for whom he arranged a rewrite on THE YELLOW SUBMARINE, and whose LOVE STORY Flaxman refused to market because he considered the script so hackneyed it was embarrassing.

Flaxman was certainly unusual. Normally you get no editing of any significance from an agent.

They don't have the time, or talent, to edit you, and what you usually get from an agent is three submissions, the first one with great enthusiasm, the second one with some restraint, and the third with careful hesitation. After that, your script is dead.

Unless of course, you wait two years, change the title, the character names and the opening scene, and get a new agent.

An agent is, however, your window on the world out there, the funnel through which you contact the studios, the networks and the major players in the game, and the one through which they contact you, and here's another never, never, never.

Never underestimate the power of an agent. I learned that one the hard way.

With Flaxman gone and BULLITT scoring unexpectedly huge theatrical grosses, making my score two for two, and my status A-list star times two, and me living in Massachusetts and having no idea of anything other than the good THE THO-MAS CROWN AFFAIR and BULLITT reviews and the money I was collecting, the William Morris office had a prob-lem,—what to do with me. I had been fired off BULLITT for "creative differences", a euphemism for my bad manners in tell-ing the director what I thought of his ideas about the woman character and his rape of my powerhouse ending. I was difficult, nouveau arrogant, with an independent income and career as a lawyer and private investor, and a delight in confrontation. That was the role Abe Lastfogel had written for me and I was playing it to a "t", or rather a "T" for Trustman "T".

On the other hand, McQueen regarded me as his. "He knows me, I don't know how, but he knows me," he would tell anyone who would listen, "and I don't care if he is a son-of-a-bitch, so is everyone in this town who is anyone, he's mine, and I want him!".

Stan Kamen, head of the William Morris theatrical division, was Steve McQueen's agent. McQueen had his heart set on making a racing car picture focused on Le Mans. They had a script with multiple problems, and the studios were leery of the project, a disaster in the making. Now if Kamen could get me to write it, and the script was a flop, that might kill several birds with one big stone, ending the project once and for all and killing off McQueen's perverse one-writer fascination. Kamen phoned me and I was flattered by the call. Imagine, having Stan Kamen as my agent!

I arrived in Los Angeles full of enthusiasm, my ever-expanding ego stoked by the treatment I received, first class American Airlines, a limo to the airport and of course, from the airport in Los Angeles to my usual bungalow at the Beverly Hills, a rented Mercedes, a lavish expense account, and lots of pictures, papers, and scripts about Le Mans which I devoured in advance of the meeting. Everyone couldn't have been nicer.

We met at Steve's home again.

It took an hour for me to understand the nature and depth of the problem: Steve. Steve had his own story idea. What the hell, actors often have story ideas, you listen, you agree, or purport to agree, and go off to your computer and do your own thing and when you deliver weeks have passed and no one remembers what was said at the meeting. I did know my man, however, and that wasn't going to work this time.

Steve's story was about a loser.

I tried. "In THE GREAT ESCAPE, you win. In SAND PEBBLES, you die at the end, and your audience loves you and doesn't want you to die at the end, so the picture fails to do the business it should. THOMAS CROWN wins. Frank BULLITT wins. Steve McQueen is now the top of the heap, with a salary in the millions and all sorts of profit points because he gives the audience what they want. They want to see him win-ning!"

I even delivered the speech well, smiling, with enthusiasm and real feeling.

No dice. Steve's hero was going to lose.

"Steve, please. We took each other to the top of the heap."

He shook his head.

Kamen was glaring at me.

Oh oh. I had made a big mistake. Steve had taken me to the top of the heap, not the other way around, and what the hell was I saying? How could I get out of this?

I became agreeable, sort of. "Look, you're the star, you can do what you want, but you're my hero, I want you to win, I can't do this with you losing."

McQueen shook his head. Kamen scowled. That ended the meeting.

Kamen drove me back to the hotel, calling me a stupid son-of-a-bitch, telling me he had made me, and he could take me down, I had embarrassed him with his most important client, he would never, never, forgive or forget, and I would never work in this town again.

I laughed. That "you'll never work in this town again" line was the punch line of so many Hollywood stories. Besides, the man was bitterly disappointed and angry with me, and clearly didn't mean what he was saying.

When he dropped me off, I gave him some advice. "Look," I told him, "It's Steve. I know the man. He says that himself, I know him. And I think he has a death wish about this racing car thing. He'll fire ten writers, ten directors, his partner, his lawyer, his agent and his wife, and die in a flaming car crash on the last day of principal photography, and I don't want to be the first writer to get the axe, and I don't want to see it happen to Steve."

Kamen drove off, tires screeching.

As it happened, I was both right and wrong. Much of what I predicted came to pass. The first director selected, a young Spielberg, was rejected by the studio. "Echhh. TV." The second director, Lucas? "No. Too short." Meaning too short physically, by the way, go figure that one. Relyea? He can produce and assistant direct. They went on location with John Sturgis.

And with six writers, count 'em, six, each working in a separate trailer on a separate script, without any agreement as to the movie they were making. Relyea wanted one man, one love, one race, one time. McQueen wanted a racing car documentary and was fascinated with wrecks, big ones. Every day they shot racing footage, car A passing car B, while the writers toiled away and Sturgis waited for a conference on the scripts that never came. One day, in exasperation, Relyea complained to the studio executive on the set, "This is out of control! We're losing it!"

The next plane brought the entire studio executive team and the plane after that arrived with the top brass from William Morris. The studio took over the picture, telling them to pick one script, any one of the scripts, get down to work and shoot it. McQueen looked at them coldly and took off for two weeks in Morocco, washing his hands creatively of the whole thing. He would stand where they told him, do what they told him, say what they told him, collect his pay and go home. It was no longer his picture.

Sturgis quit. They threatened him, telling him he would never work again. He flew home and was employed on another picture as soon as he got off the airplane. The studio hired a self-proclaimed Harvard alumnus who was unknown to the Harvard alumni office, wore a Phi Beta Kappa key on the set, and had directed several unreleasable pictures. They neglected to tell Relyea that they had hired the man, and when he found out, he also quit. Steve never spoke again to Relyea, his friend and partner for many years. Steve fired the William Morris office. There was even a car crash on the last day of principal photography, just as I had predicted, but Steve was not seriously injured. His divorce came in another two years.

The picture, LE MANS, was, to say the least, not a conspicuous success.

And I was wrong about Stan Kamen. For five years, my phone never rang. I never got an offer, a single one. Most writers live off assignments, and I didn't even know what an assignment was when David Begelman recruited me five years later as an ICM client. Hottest screenwriter in the business, top of the heap, and for all practical purposes, dead and gone.

Begelman thought it was hilarious. Kamen was listed as my agent with the Writers Guild, all the inquiries had come to him, and I never knew what was going on. Didn't I care enough to ask someone? David said.

I couldn't answer the question.

Back to you: Your agent can get your script read, or pretend-read. That is one of his primary functions.

But your script had better be submitted together with the commitment of a hot bankable element.

13

THE RESPONSES TO A FORCED READ

Naked scripts do sometimes happen. How can you tell if yours is happening?

Let's suppose you get a forced read. For example, somehow you do get an agent, and he submits your script, naked, with no bankable element attached, to a bored, harassed, overworked do-nothing executive whose room is littered with unread scripts, and insists the executive get the script read, the executive sends your screenplay our for coverage and by some miracle responds to what he sees as a possible pitch line for the project despite the negative coverage. He gets so steamed up over his pitch line, his creation, that he decides to call you. What does he say?

There are three possibilities, the quarter Nelson, the half Nelson and the full Nelson, named after the Director Ralph Nelson who first described the phenomenon.

The executive may give you the quarter Nelson, a statement that he has your script, thanks, he'll read it over the weekend. What he means is that he has read it, or more likely the coverage, and likes something about it, and is going to organize the political forces in his shop to get others interested in the project so if they move with it, there will be shared responsibility if the project flops. You must express friendliness and pleasure at his kindness and courtesy and write down whatever words he uses to describe the project so you can use them in your pitch if the project goes forward.

He may give you the half Nelson, a statement that he has read it and likes it but it needs work. What that means is that he absolutely loves it, he has gotten others in the studio interested in the project, they are going to brim with enthusiasm and stall in an effort to option your script, and they are already shopping for other writers to rewrite your script. The half Nelson is good news but never, never, never sell an option. If you do, you will soon be out of the project, it is likely to be rewritten endlessly, it is unlikely ever to get made, and if it should by some miracle be made, you will in all likelihood hate it and you may not even receive screenplay credit. More later about credits.

You should tell your agent you want to sell, not option your screenplay, you want at the very least Writers Guild minimum against a big price if the picture is made plus net points which will be writer points, and those are always net profit points and unlikely to mean anything, plus the first two rewrites, and you want to be paid in addition at least WGA minimum for each of the rewrites. You probably won't get all of that, but you may get the bulk of it and if you do, you will be around long enough to meet the key people, and it is always possible that there will be another miracle and your rewrites may catch the fancy of one of the key elements.

A digression: I collected net profit points on both THE THOMAS CROWN AFFAIR and BULLITT, but studio accounting got more creative after that and I am sure there are some but I don't know of any net profits participations in the last 30 years. The THOMAS CROWN AFFAIR remake cost about $60 million and has done box office of $100 million but it somehow shows a net loss of $90 million and I am the proud owner of a 5% interest in that net loss, which is fortunately non-contributory. MGM/UA is keeping their books both accurately and in accordance with industry practice and even if they were not, there would be no point in suing them. There is no point in ever suing one of the movie studios, as Art Buchwald discovered after his COMING TO AMERICA lawsuit, where his million dollar recovery was balanced by years of effort and an equal amount in legal fees.

Back to the full Nelson: The studio executive may tell you that it costs too much. That is the best news you can get. That means the studio is definitely going to buy it, they are willing to pay a premium, they will make a big fuss over you, and it will be months before you discover that there are other writers on the project. But that doesn't matter. You are the flavor of the month! You are in, at last!

You have sold your screenplay!

They are going to make your movie!

14

THE PACKAGE STALL

Next your project will go through the package stall.

That can last for months, if not years, as the studio and producer try to assemble the necessary bankable director and stars. Remember what I told you about the art form being the package? Here's where you discover why.

To begin with, pretty much every producer is surrounded by a staff, spouse, lover, agent and manager who want him to do something else.

Every director and actor is surrounded by a staff, spouse, lover, agent and manager who want him to do something else in which they represent other elements or have some sort of larger interest, and they protect access to the director and actor as if that access is the crown jewels. It is in fact their crown jewel, their lifeblood, their money. The producer and studio may have to deal with some or all of those people in addition to the director and each actor in order to get commitments. Deal in this context means persuade, somehow, by whatever it takes.

The packaging process is made even more difficult by the fact that the average Hollywood director and actor has an attention span of 72 hours, and you usually recruit with both the pitch and the identity of the other elements already committed, so if you cannot nail down all the elements plus the studio approval to finance and distribute within a 72-hour period, some key element is likely to drop out, and maybe not bother to tell you that he has dropped out. Once one element drops out, all the other elements will feel free to drop out.

In defense of the system, however, a movie is a cooperative endeavor in which producer, writer, director, stars and editor all have a role to play, and unless the full cast has been assembled and approved, why should anyone commit millions to the project?

Okay, you've been lucky. You sold a script. Miraculously, it has been packaged and the key elements are meaningfully committed, some of them pay or play, meaning they are going to get paid whether or not the picture is made.

The picture is almost certainly going to get made.

Now it really gets ugly. You are entering what is known in the trade as development hell.

15

REWRITER HEAVEN, WRITER DEVELOPMENT HELL

Whether or not they admit it, each studio, network or cable company has its own list of preferred writers. They feel more comfortable putting up the money if one of their own writers has blessed the script.

Further, every key element, and his staff, spouse, lover, agent and manager has a brother, sister, cousin or lover who is a screenwriter, and yours is a go project, meaning that screenwriters throughout the town are just dying to get hired to rewrite your script. That starts before the production start date and, even more destructive, it continues until the movie is wrapped, and sometimes even thereafter.

It isn't just money that the writers want, although rewriting is very, very highly paid, and the rewriters will frequently be paid more than you got paid for your original script and your rewrites. What they want most of all is a chance to get a screen credit, and the residual payments derived from screen credit. Indeed, according to the late Ernie Tidyman, who wrote the first SHAFT and twice rewrote me, the objective of a rewriter is change for the sake of claiming credit, and not change in order to improve the script.

As Ernie laid the rewrite process out for me, first you rewrite every word of the dialogue, changing the words even if you keep the sense of the speech. Then you change the beginning and ending of the picture. Then you change the structure, moving the key scenes here and there, cutting some, and adding others. Then you change the characters, eliminating some and adding others. Then you rewrite every single page until you can claim that you wrote more than half of it. Then you ask everybody on the project from the studio go-fer through the agent for the second male lead's lover for their suggestions, and they will all give you suggestions. They want to feel creative. The less creative they are, the more they will wish to feel creative. You nod happily, pretend to consider seriously all their suggestions, no matter how idiotic, and adopt whatever suggestions you can, recognizing their deep emotional need to make a creative contribution to a go picture so they can tell people ever after see that? Remember that? That was their idea.

When you have made all the changes you feel are politically desirable, you hand in your rewrite and move on, making way for the next rewriter.

And there will be another rewriter.

Illogically, in a sense unbelievably, rewrites frequently continue with varying intensity throughout the entire production. By then, the original writer is gone, long gone.

Some of the very best directors have been among the most profligate users of multiple writers. John Sturgis, for example, had to keep taking the script apart, over and over and over again, exhausting and replacing the writers. On THE GREAT ESCAPE there were a dozen different writers and, with only half a day's shooting left to finish principal photography, Sturgis could be seen in his trailer, huddled with the final writer, uncredited John Gay, shuffling 3 x 5 cards, reshuffling, reorganizing, rewriting.

William Wyler had similar habits. He had a huge poster in his office showing the endless procession scene from the TEN COMMANDMENTS and uncredited writer Wendell Mayes, there for a conference on CHIDREN'S HOUR, deadpanned, "Those are the writers he used on BEN HUR".

Actors turned director go the other way. George C. Scott used to call himself "Candy Ass" for speaking his one line then returning to his chair for the rest of the day. He made certain that would never happen when he got to direct. He showed up for THE SAVAGE IS LOOSE with a huge 3-ring binder, with every shot specified to the last detail, eliciting the comment from a crew with nothing to do except follow his astonishingly explicit instructions, "How much do we have to pay you back for the privilege of working here?" Scott refused to deviate in any way from the script.

The movie was not a success.

Duke Wayne—John Wayne to you—and no, I never met him either—was one of the best organized directors of all time. Communicating with actors may not have been his forte but efficiency clearly was. His golden rule: shoot the script. The weather changed? Shoot the script. The actor was sick? Shoot the script. The writer might be there, and frequently was, but there were never changes in the script. The Duke produced, starred in and directed THE ALAMO, and is rumored to have borrowed the $14 million budget from Murchison, in effect financing the movie personally.

It took 15 years to recoup its costs and it, too, was not a success.

But the production was efficient.

Even where the movie is a success, the sole writer may well not share in the plaudits. Ernie Lehman was the sole writer on WEST SIDE STORY, on which virtually everyone got an

Academy Award except for the leading man, leading lady, and Ernie. He didn't even get a nomination, the general impression being that all he did was adapt the Arthur Laurents book for the play. Not true. Lehman did far more than that. And reaped not the slightest credit.

Buck Henry had a clever solution to this. On THE DAY OF THE DOLPHIN, he is rumored to have agreed with everything Mike Nichols said, staying close to the throne being an effective technique for precluding other writers, at least on a set where the director himself was also a brilliant writer. The cost of work permits in the Bahamas varies according to the importance of the position being filled. The Best Boy, being important, cost $450 for his permit. The writer permit cost $50.

LE MANS was one of the extreme cases of a multiple-writer-on-the-set shambles, presided over while it lasted by the ever-patient John Sturgis.

Rewrites can continue after production is wrapped and even after the answer print. MGM/UA continued rewriting and reshooting the recent SUPERNOVA long after Walter Hill delivered his director's cut, getting further and further away from Walter's vision of the movie and the script.

16

MAY HEAVEN PROTECT THE WORKING WRITER

Heaven may, but the Writers Guild will not, protect you.

I do not have the statistics but I believe that a majority of the voting members of the guild make their living rewriting other writers' scripts. Although they do not declare it, the guild tacitly encourages rewriting as it makes more work and more pay for more writers, which is sensible if you take the broad view.

Even more disappointing, the credit arbitration process is not helpful to the original writers of scripts. In the old days, 75 senior citizens did the arbitrations, they all knew the score, you never submitted a statement or brief or asked for an oral argument and somehow it always came out right, particularly if you wrote the original script.

Today there are close to 3,000 would-be arbitrators, the average age is under 30, they all know each other, and despite the guild's insistence that the evaluations are completely anonymous, in many cases the arbitrators know perfectly well who did which draft of the script. If you are an old-timer and live out of town, you can just forget it. You don't have a chance in most situations to get an arbitrated credit for your script.

Yes, there are exceptions. The remake of THE THOMAS CROWN AFFAIR had the same plot, the same characters, the same structure, and much of the same dialogue. They changed Boston to New York, the two bank robberies which would have worked to two art robberies which wouldn't have worked, and added an epilogue which I hated, converting a romantic movie about two hotshots who were madly in love but couldn't possibly make it together into a they-all-lived-happily-ever-after. Overall, it was my script, and in the old days I would have received sole writing credit, with one of the eight rewriters, count them, eight, possibly getting an additional dialogue credit or at the most, a junior story credit.

The studio proposed giving me no credit at all, the posters were printed giving me no credit at all, and the film was previewed with me getting no credit at all. Oh, well, what the hell, game over, hopeless. Unknown to me, however, the Minimum Basic Agreement requires an automatic arbitration in the event of a remake, with the script for the original movie being entered as the first script. Credits are supposed to be based on plot, mine, characters, mine, structure, mine, and dialogue, partially mine, so it was embarrassing, going on outrageous, to give me no credit at all. The arbitrators cleverly compromised, giving me story credit. Others got screenplay credit.

I laughed.

Two years later the Guild fined the studio $7,000 for the original posters and screenings and, quoting Ben Hogan, I delivered my favorite speech, "Thanks for the check."

P.S. People always ask so I might as well say that I thought the remake was pretty good. I enjoyed the art robberies enormously despite some logical anomalies, I thought the performances were great, just great, I admired the work of the director and despite the awful ending, on balance I thoroughly enjoyed the picture.

I have written a contract clause to protect the writer of an original and if I am ever a star again, I may very well get it into a contract. It provides that I get more money if they hire another writer, even more if he gets any junior credit, more still if he gets senior story or screenplay credit, and lots more if I get no credit. A good idea, but the clause has never been tested, and if it ever should be tested, the Writers Guild may very well intervene and argue that the clause should be invalid as inconsistent with the policy of the Writers Guild to encourage the hiring of more writers. If that should happen, I would be outraged but I would not litigate it. Only the wealthiest can afford litigation in the movie business.

17

THE PRELIMINARIES

Fine. Now that you understand the business, how do you sell your script?

The first thing you MUST do is create your own pitch. Write it. Practice selling it. First ask the mirror, are you projecting the necessary enthusiasm? If not, it needs more work.

When you are ready, practice on people. Are the people on whom you are inflicting the sell listening intently or with amused boredom? Are they galvanized by your enthusiasm? Are they just dying to see the movie? Ask them to tell you about the movie. Are they feeding back to you the same enthusiasm in the very same words?

If you are not getting exactly the response you need, go back to your computer and rewrite your pitch.

Your movie is going to sell and get made—or not—on the basis of your pitch. Your delivery of your pitch. You cannot rely on anyone else, certainly not a star actor as one unhappy writer learned watching a flavor of the moment pitch his script to an eager studio head and a curious John Huston. Huston listened with mounting horror to a litany of inappropriate literary and philosophical references, and when the actor finally paused, expectantly beaming, Huston turned to the studio head. "How could you do this to me?" he said. He then left.

The picture was directed by someone else, and it was a box-office disappointment.

The second thing you must do is read your beginning in the cold light of a new day several weeks after you have finished your script and ask yourself whether your opening ten pages (1) seize the attention of a reader, (2) establish an interesting milieu, (3) introduce at least one character whom the reader likes, and (4) present some sort of problem or situation so the reader will want to turn pages to find out what happens next.

If you have any doubts about any of that, rewrite until you are absolutely sure and before you dare show the script.

A substantial percentage of the people who read your screenplay will not go beyond the first ten pages unless all four of those requirements are satisfied and if even one of them is missing, they are highly likely to toss your script.

I cannot fault this ten-page filter as I once admitted the chosen 14 of 82 applicants for the screenwriting course I taught at Harvard based on the submission of the first ten pages of a script. I thought I could tell the talent that way and I have never regretted any of the choices. On the other hand, the writer of the 15th screenplay, the best of those rejected, went on to become a highly successful screenwriter and has received at least two Academy Award screenplay nominations; I voted for both of them. I have never met the man and he has never forgiven me; I keep getting the message from people who know both of us.

And now we come to the most important element of any movie script: the ending. In a sense, the end is the beginning.

I once gave a Steuben glass masterpiece with those words inscribed on it to my first genius agent, John Flaxman. The ending of THE THOMAS CROWN AFFAIR which he wheedled, browbeat and forced out of me was the key to the success of that picture and the key to my movie success.

Before you show your script to anyone, please please please check your ending.

There are, I maintain, only four possible movie endings. Yes, I know that sounds ridiculous. I believe deep in my secret flower that it should be wrong, it must be wrong, so I have tried hard to test it.

I tried it out on friends in the business for ten months and no one, unbelievably no one, could come up with a fifth ending. Next I published it in an article in the WASHINGTON POST, challenging the millions of their readers to come up with a fifth ending, and instead of the dozens of responses I expected, no one, not one single reader of the WASHINGTON POST, wrote in to suggest that there was a fifth ending.

So let's assume for the moment that there are only four.

What are the four possible endings?

The fourth most successful ending is repeating a joke, something that has elicited a laugh at least once, and preferably twice, earlier in the picture. The audience will experience the joy of recognition and the pleasure of laughter and will leave the theater happy.

The third most successful ending is existential and pleases critics and academics. We learn that the same thing is going to happen all over again. We chuckle and feel philosophical and intellectually profound.

The second most successful ending is the surprise finale tying everything together and making the whole movie somehow make sense. We feel full, satisfied and intellectually challenged.

The most successful ending has two elements. The hero,—someone we care for, someone who wants and needs something we want him to have, but cannot possibly get, —somehow does get it in an unanticipated fashion. This will send us out of the theater feeling happy, satisfied and somehow complete. The ending is even better if, at the same time, the villain is punished as the villain deserves, preferably in exactly the same fashion in which the villain has inflicted harm on others. That will make us feel just great.

If you don't have one of those ending, please please please keep rewriting your script.

18

THE FIRST SOUL SEARCH

Okay, now that you have a script and your pitch, before you go any further, examine your soul. You do have a soul, and before you subject it to the movie business, I suggest three important soul searches.

First, do you want to be a director and producer, and NOT just a screenwriter, or at least can you convincingly purport to want to be a director and producer? You are flirting with an industry where actors are star celebrities and, during their minutes in the sunshine, the tickets to heavy-duty financing, but the directors are the kings, the producers are the powers behind the thrones and the generals that keep the armies moving, and the screenwriters are considered fungible commodities with time-limited shelf lives, even those who are highly respected.

Yes, there are highly successful screenwriters who remain as such, and sometimes they continue to work regularly at significant salaries even after failed sorties into the limelight as directors, and brief participations as producers, but they are rare. Although there are no statistics, in my admittedly limited experience those screenwriters who make it known that they really want to be directors and producers tend to be taken a bit more seriously, almost as if screenwriting is an appropriate career for the very young and inexperienced and, as you grow, you are expected to turn director and producer.

Further, you should be aware of the La Brea tar pit phenomenon, the all-too-common Hollywood talent trap. In many, many cases, young talent has one success, and perhaps two, followed by pictures which are significantly less than a success, then a change of agent and manager, a slow but relentless drift from hot to toe stubber and no longer Big, to disappointed, disconsolate, depressed and out of work, becoming progressively more peripheral, and ending up with nose pressed to the glass, ever hopeful but increasingly bitter at being replaced by younger new and fresh flavors of the month who are no more talented but somehow get the work. Hollywood is a town that chews up its young people and spits them into the tar pit.

The transition from writer to director, and better still, to director and producer, may well be the best way to continue to find that all-important work.

Frank Pierson is a fascinating illustration of the evolution of a superb writer into a better director and producer. After bursting triumphantly onto the scene with screenplays for CAT BAL-LOU, THE HAPPENING and the COOL HAND LUKE disaster, he wrote and directed THE LOOKING GLASS WAR in the 1960's; he wrote THE ANDERSON TAPES and DOG DAY AFTERNOON and wrote and directed A STAR IS BORN and KING OF THE GYPSIES in the 1970's. I loved KING OF THE GYPSIES. I thought it was one the very best pictures I saw that year, but apparently the powers that were did not agree and for his career it seems to have been a crusher. Pierson's writing credits consist solely of HAYWIRE for TV in 1980 and nothing else until IN COUNTRY and PRESUMED INNOCENT in 1989 and 1990. His sole directing credit was one of the Alfred Hitchcock Presents installments in 1985. Then, in one of Hollywood's rare but well-deserved miracles, he was reincarnated as a leading television director with SOME-BODY HAS TO SHOOT THE PICTURE in 1990, followed thereafter by CITIZEN COHN, SIEGE AT WOUNDED

KNEE, TRUMAN, DIRTY PICTURES, CONSPIRACY and SOLDIER'S GIRL, all of them among the classiest features ever seen on TV. Although I am one of his great admirers, I have never met or spoken to the man so I have no idea why, with his career at its peak, he hasn't had a movie writing or directing credit in 22 years. Can the studios possibly consider him too old despite his recent series of brilliant television films, or would he rather not work with them?

Success for a non-director, non-producer writer can take years, many years, even if you are a huge talent and spend your entire adult life in Los Angeles, and often turns on the evolution into director and producer. I met Curtis Hanson in 1970 when he was trying to make a movie from the song, TAMBOURINE MAN. He was 25 and a struggling screenwriter who wanted to be a director with one credit, THE DUNWICH HORROR. He got his first chance with THE SWEET KILL in 1972, which he wrote, produced and directed. It was not a success and he vanished for years, writing and producing a Canadian feature late in the decade and writing WHITE DOG and directing LITTLE DRAGONS, which he also executive produced, and LOSIN' IT in the early 1980's. I looked him up again in the early 1990's after THE BEDROOM WINDOW and BAD INFLUENCE both of which I liked enormously. Why hadn't he done more? He shrugged. It was tough to get his act together. He was going to stay with thrillers. They were his best shot at making it,—and he did, with THE HAND THAT ROCKS THE CRADLE, THE RIVER WILD and L.A. CONFIDENTIAL, a classic of the noir genre, and one which got an Academy Award Best Director nomination for Curtis and a Best Actress award for Kim Basinger and was Kevin Spacey's and Russell Crowe's breakthrough picture. Curtis' next picture, WONDER BOYS, did some business and last year he had the extraordinary 8 MILE in the theatres. He has been a credited producer on all his pictures starting with L.A. CONFIDENTIAL. Curtis has one serious problem in the business: he is nice, a good person, definitely not a monster. He even returns my phone calls, some of the time, despite the fact that he is by now definitely and permanently A-list.

What is a producer? A complete producer obtains the rights to the script or property, nurses it to the stage of the shooting script, assembles the necessary director, actor and actress package, negotiates the financing and distribution deal, supervises production and post production, makes certain that all the elements are working together constructively if not in harmony, shelters them from foolish and irritating intervention from incompetent studio executive would-be creatives, and rides herd on the project through exhibition and all the other forms of exploitation.

The perfect producer, in the opinion of director Norman Jewison, was the late Harold Mirisch who showed up on the set one day and said, "What can I do to help?"

The director, cast and crew nearly wept.

There are producers, executive producers, associate producers, assistant producers, assistant executive producers, co-producers of various kinds, and probably a few more species that at the moment I can't remember. There are 16 producers and producing company credits on NARC, as I write this playing in the theatres.

I once saw a "Financier" credit on a Sissy Spacek picture and the audience cognoscenti present snickered derisively. I did not. It seemed to me that it was one of the rare honest credits I have seen.

All of the producers, with the exception of line producers, are people who have had sufficient input into the packaging and financing to demand a screen credit and money, and they may have had no role whatsoever in the making of the picture. Line producers are the people who actually manage the making of the picture, and for some reason they tend to have less status and receive less money than most other forms of producer.

Being the line producer is frequently thankless, almost always under-compensated, and always Catch-22 highly dangerous. The line-producer is charged with making sure the picture is finished on time, and on budget. Those objectives are often inconsistent. The studio executives who set those objectives do not see them as inconsistent, and do not relish being told they are inconsistent. Line producers are easy to blame and the studios are notoriously unforgiving of line producers.

Item: The studio sent Jim Henderling to Cairo and Alexandria as line producer on CLEOPATRA where he discovered in the first three days that many of the business arrangements had been arranged in a manner that may be called euphemistically "Egyptian". He reported this and was promptly fired.

Sometimes you can't win. Item: The studio sent Bob Relyea to Southeast Asia as line producer on THE DEER HUNTER.

He was eating fish heads on a jungle mountain in the rain when he learned that he and the director were having a little "creative disagreement". Back in Pennsylvania, the director was building the set for a motel alongside an existing real motel. Bob considered this a bit extravagant. He phoned the studio and asked if they had authorized the build. They had. Bob promptly quit, on principle. It was his job to control the spending. It cost him an Oscar, quitting. The picture won the Best Picture Academy Award. There were four producers credited on the film and all of them went home with their statues in hand. All Bob would have had to do to get one for himself was to shut his mouth and go along for the ride, ignoring his responsibility for cost control. When the picture is a winner, nobody cares. As for the triumphant director of THE DEER HUNTER, he escalated even further his next time out and nearly bankrupted United Artists with his uncontrolled spending.

A word of advice for line producers: it is a very risky career choice.

Making deals is safer than making movies and much more financially rewarding, even if you are extremely talented. This is well illustrated by the movie life story of the most brilliant and passionately committed line producer I ever met.

19

THE SHORT HAPPY MOVIE LIFE OF HARRISON STARR, LINE PRODUCER

Harrison was the most talented line producer of all those I ever met.

He is the epitome of the "one of", one of a kind, and they break the mold after. A pixie with tangled curly hair, flashing blue eyes, an engaging grin and the build and strength of the black belt I think he once was and maybe still is, you can—and I have done it—phone him in a restaurant by telling the person who answers the phone to "Look for Puck, as in MIDSUMMER NIGHT'S DREAM, and you'll know him when you see him."

Young, fiercely energetic, imaginative, understanding, quick to learn and just as quick to fight, he was the outstanding production manager and line producer of the 1960's New York independent film scene. United Artists had successfully established the studio-without-a-studio trend, financing and distributing without owning a movie lot or shouldering the crew, real estate and other overhead incidental costs, and by the mid-1960's Columbia was attempting the same sort of thing with a small, separate division. After a 1961 baptism on MAD DOG COLL, Harrison was production manager for United Artists and Arthur Penn on THE MIRACLE WORKER the following year and stepped from that frying pan into THE CARDINAL fire for Columbia and Otto Preminger a year later.

He was present at the incident in Vienna in St. Stefan's Square which some consider a defining moment in Preminger's career. Preminger was unquestionably a wonderful producer, a magnificent field general, terrific at running a set but lacking in patience and people skills and given to rages when frustrated as he sometimes was by his own directorial artistic limitations. There they all were in the huge city square with half the power grid of the city tied up, every generator in the country they could beg, borrow or steal, and 3,000 crew, cast and extras milling around, and Preminger could not get the effect he wished. Perhaps he could not get it right in his head. He moved people and equipment, moved them again, tried run-throughs, and still it somehow didn't work. He tried it again and again and eventually exploded in frustration, directing his fury at an extra who had not walked as Preminger wished. Rabid in his loss of temper, he railed on and on until English Assistant Director, Gerry O'Hara, politely interrupted.

"I'm sorry, sir, but that's not the man's fault. I told him to walk there."

Preminger turned on O'Hara, and again raged on and on, until O'Hara quietly handed his microphone to another assistant director and walked off the set with the words, "I'll leave."

3,000 people fell silent as O'Hara walked the 40 paces to the edge of the square. O'Hara was not only a good man, but one of the very best in the crew, and all of them present knew it. 3,000 people, all motionless, watched it happen.

As O'Hara was about to disappear into the crowd off the square, Preminger cleared his throat and bellowed, "Mr. O'Hara! Get back to your duties!"

O'Hara paused. Turned. Considered. It was as close to an apology as he was going to get and more than Preminger was thought able to give. O'Hara walked slowly back to the other A.D. and recovered his microphone.

The shoot continued.

But the scene was disappointing.

After a short stint in Tennessee on THE FOOL KILLER directed by Servando Gonzalez, Harrison went back to work for Arthur Penn on MICKEY ONE for Columbia Pictures. It was one of the first big studio small pictures to be made in Chicago and the city welcomed the New Yorkers. They were even able to use Louis Malle's French camera man. The Chicago unions permitted it. The New York unions would never have permitted it and there would have been no point in asking.

Harrison was able to make unexpectedly favorable location deals, and they were soon under budget. Harrison was about to report that to Columbia when Bill Schneider, the studio representative on the set, stopped him.

"Never tell a studio that you are that far under budget."

"But we are, and I'm proud of it—"

"Don't. Something will go wrong, it always does, and the moment you tell them you're dropping behind, they'll hold you responsible. They'll be disappointed and it'll be all your fault. Until you wrap on the very last day, you are never under budget. Got it?"

"I hear you."

"Say 'thanks'."

"Thanks."

"Remember, it's never the director's fault and of course, it's never the actor's fault, and if the picture makes money they both win, but the production manager never wins if he goes over budget."

It proved to be a long shoot. Hurd Hatfield of DORIAN GREY fame was difficult, to say the least, and Warren Beatty was feeling his oats, insisting on 40 takes, sometimes 50 takes, but Penn was able to be patient. There was room in the budget.

It was a good if not an outstanding film although it never did the hoped-for box office.

In the course of the production, Harrison had two visits from French celebrity auteur directors among whom his reputation had rapidly spread as one of the rare Americans in production who understood the European artistic esprit, someone on this side of the Atlantic who was truly different. No picture resulted from the visits but each time he learned something. And the existence of a Harrison Starr, who understood their cinema, and understood them, was in my opinion one of the principal reasons several celebrity foreign directors decided to try their hands at American, if not Hollywood, work.

Francois Truffaut came to Chicago to discuss the possible production in Canada of FAHRENHEIT 451. Harrison was honored and flattered and the two instantly took to each other. They went for a long walk along the Lake Shore and Truffaut said he was thinking of hiring Hurd Hatfield for one of the leading roles. Harrison groaned. "He's been a real problem for Arthur Penn. Hurd is just so difficult."

Truffaut continued to walk and finally said, "Yes. The really good ones usually are."

The picture was made in London and, much to Truffaut's regret, Harrison declined to manage the production. The

English full studio crew was not particularly helpful to the world-famous auteur Frenchman.

The next phone call came from Jean-Luc Godard. Benton and Newman, who were then unknowns, and two would-be producers who lived on Central Park West, had sent Godard their BONNY AND CLYDE script. Godard thought it was wonderful. He asked Harrison to meet with him and the would-be producers in New York. Godard flew in from Paris, and Harrison came in from Chicago on a Sunday of rest for MICKEY ONE. The producers were friendly and so was Godard until he asked his first question. The answer was smiles and nonsense. Godard shifted in his chair and asked a second question. He got a similar response, more smiles and nonsense.

"Excuse me," said Jean-Luc Godard and went out of the room.

The producers continued to chat with Harrison for a few minutes and then fell silent, waiting for Godard to return.

He didn't.

"Where is he? In the bathroom?" they finally asked.

"Gone," said Harrison.

"He left?"

"Yes."

"What? How come?"

"You don't understand," Harrison told them, "and you never will, and you'll never make a movie with Jean-Luc Godard. As for the script, good luck to you. I still think it's a good one."

Harrison kept the script with him.

Back in Chicago, it was lying on his desk when Warren Beatty came in between MICKEY ONE takes with nothing to do and started leafing through it.

"Can I make a copy?" Warren asked.

Harrison said sure, and Warren took the script. He returned the original the following day.

Two years later Warren phoned. "How'd you like to make a picture in Texas?" Warren said.

Harrison was delighted. "What is it?" he asked.

"BONNY AND CLYDE."

What goes around, comes around.

They went to Texas together and of course it would work. Harrison prepared a budget, and knowing Warren from the 50-take MICKEY ONE, he padded it a bit to get extra shooting time and asked David Picker at United Artists to approve a budget of $1,750,000. Picker was under pressure to keep budgets down and offered $1,500,000. Harrison made a mistake and held at $1,600,000.

Warren, who was very smart and could feel himself on the verge of stardom, went to Abe Lastfogel, the head of the William Morris office, and told him to set it up somewhere else or he would leave the agency. Lastfogel knew which side his bread was buttered on and called in a favor at Warner Bros. Warner Bros., who hated the script, and did not much like Warren, approved the project. A year later they had themselves a runaway hit. Arthur Penn directed but Harrison was unavailable to produce.

He was off preparing a movie with Akira Kurosawa, the dream of a lifetime.

The movie was going to be THE RUNAWAY TRAIN, an idea Kurosawa found fascinating. They needed a stretch of straight railroad in snow and prospected for locations in various places in southern Canada and northern New England, then adjourned to Japan to shoot a test scene.

Of all the people with whom Harrison ever worked, Kurosawa knew the most, about everything. His knowledge of the craft was more than outstanding, it was breathtaking. He was tall for a Japanese, quiet, soft spoken, a presence, a sensei, a master of men. Being with Kurosawa in Japan was like being with the King of the World, which, in that world, Kurosawa truly was.

After months of preparation, they went for the test shoot. The equipment was old, which the Japanese found embarrassing, but it was serviceable for the scene they planned to shoot. They spent the full first day setting it up. The second day was more of the same. The third day was a repetition of the first two, with Kurosawa making slight adjustments in people and equipment, never quite satisfied, never getting quite the shot he had in mind. Harrison started to worry. How could he do a budget for a director like this? How could they control an American crew with a director who was endlessly tinkering? At 4:00 pm on the third day, Kurosawa suddenly said, "Okay," and they shot the scene. One take, ten minutes, and it was done. The moment came, he got it, and it was perfect, just what he wished. It was like a cobra striking.

Unfortunately, the financier went broke and the picture was abandoned for nearly 20 years. Andrei Konchalovsky directed it in 1985 for Golan-Globus and MGM with Jon Voight, Eric Roberts and Rebecca de Mornay. I saw it but Harrison didn't.

Harrison then returned to the United States and produced the sort of production he knew cold, RACHEL RACHEL with Joanne Woodward, directed by Paul Newman. He was then asked by Carlo Ponti and Michaelangelo Antonioni to line-produce Antonioni's big-time make or break Hollywood film, ZABRISKIE POINT, for which Harrison, knowledgeable and experienced, and respected by the temperamental European elite, seemed to be exactly the right person.

Maybe he was, but MGM wasn't.

Antonioni made his movies in his own head, intuitively, instinctively, and it might have worked if he had had an independent crew, small, flexible and tolerant, but that was an impossibility given the MGM situation. There was only one other picture in production on the MGM lot and that was an inexpensive movie for TV. It was otherwise a dead season with dozens of experienced people sitting around with nothing to do, angry, unemployed, worrying.

It would have been a slap in the face to MGM and the guilds and created an impossible situation had they tried to go non-union, even if experienced independents competent to deal with Antonioni's imaginative demands had been available, and that was very much in doubt. As a result, Harrison recruited an experienced MGM union crew and tried to make them work as best he and they could with a genius auteur Italian working in a foreign land and language, a Ferrarese with that town's oblique approach to people and vision of the universe in terms of flow and shading.

It was difficult for both Antonioni and the crew and a nightmare for Harrison.

The budget was adequate as was the time to prepare, and they spent much of the seven months of preparation time searching out a variety of Death Valley locations, in the course of which Harrison got his first taste of another of the problems to come in the difficulty in getting permissions.

Principal photography began on time.

It was hard, slow going from the first day with a crew who regarded the director as a crazy foreigner and had doubts about the project as a whole, and a director who was well aware that he was surrounded by suspicion. The location problems continued throughout. People who would normally have granted permission refused and some of those who said yes changed their minds and said no. The FBI was reported to be watching the shoot of an immoral, Communist sex picture on American soil. Yet the production was not without its brilliant moments.

During one of their pre-production location scouts they had come across an abandoned, derelict market, service station and theatre near Death Valley Junction. Antonioni had spotted a junked piano in a rubble pile and insisted on having it. They trucked it away and stored it with no further conversation. Seven months later they were shooting a Mojave desert motel scene where the script called for the heroine to be accosted by juvenile delinquents. Antonioni asked for the piano and in the scene as filmed, the juvenile delinquents are plucking the piano strings and eyeing the heroine like jackals. In the words of the trade, that scene sang.

A number of others didn't.

One evening, as they finished and walked off the set, Michaelangelo indicated an assistant cameraman and muttered to Harrison, "Get rid of him."

"What's the matter?"

"I can't work with him."

"It's not that easy. There's a union, there are procedures set, and we need to have a reason."

"The reason is I don't want him around."

"Why?"

"He has the evil eye."

Harrison paid the man off and fired him. The man had friends. There were repercussions. The studio blamed Harrison.

Much later it was discovered that Antonioni had been right. The man did have the evil eye—he had been an observer reporting to the FBI on the suspected dangerous Communist production.

Ultimately, the FBI did make a move.

Antonioni had an inspiration. A vision. A thousand beautiful young people, naked, making love in the desert at dawn. For years I have been telling the story as if he told Harrison at dinner one night and planned to shoot it the following morning. Good story, but that's not what happened. In fact, they had a month to prepare.

It was not the easiest scene to arrange. They could not recruit in Los Angeles because it was much too far away and the cost of transportation to Death Valley, on top of the cost of the necessary food, housing and toilet facilities, was just too much of a problem. They visited fraternities and sororities in Las Vegas, recruited a good 500 more-than-willing students and brought them to Death Valley for the shoot. Across state lines. The FBI descended on them, threatening to prosecute for bringing people for immoral purposes across state lines. Harrison was interviewed and so were several others. The threat hung over the production like a huge black cloud even though ultimately there was no prosecution.

Meanwhile, the shoot did not go well.

At dawn, they assembled the 500 beautiful young people and a massive crew, complete with wind machines,—and Harrison found himself back in St. Stefan's Square again.

Antonioni could not get the effect he wanted.

He spent the first full day making adjustments in people and equipment but it was not right.

The second day was grim. More adjustments, but it was still not right.

They tried again on the third day and Antonioni, who was reasonable, was well aware what it was costing. Finally, he lost his temper.

Shoot. Cut. Wrap.

Antonioni was not happy with the scene. He had not gotten his vision. It was painful for him in the extreme.

They went over budget, which was painful for Harrison in the extreme.

All would have been well had the picture done good business, but it failed at the box office dismally. The new MGM management tried desperately to sell the picture off. Harrison took the blame for everything. It cost him his career and his reputation.

It also cost him one of his favorite, albeit most tempestuous, marriages, to the writer Sally, daughter of Murray, Kempton. Line producing a ZABRISKIE POINT under that sort of adverse circumstances is a total time, energy and attention commitment, an all-consuming killer of any relationship requiring attention. Sally was later to publish two articles in the same issue of ESQUIRE, one on Dustin Hoffman and the other one of the most telling contributions in the literary history of militant feminism including a sentence that was so poignant that I still remember it almost verbatim after 30 years. She said she used to lie awake beside him at night wanting to hit him over the head with a frying pan, and the reason she didn't do it wasn't because she was afraid she would hurt him,—God, she would have loved to hurt him,—but because she was afraid he would leave her.

His producing career was effectively dead but there was one more nail in that coffin to come.

I was to provide it.

20

THE SECOND SOUL SEARCH

Back to you and your second soul search: Are you willing to move to Los Angeles and work the town full-time, spending every minute of every day taking breakfast, lunch, dinner and other meetings, socializing with the people, learning how to talk their language, forcing yourself to listen, forgiving all sorts of bizarre conduct and ethical lapses, putting up with the outrageous and boring, and insisting your spouse or lover do the same?

Allot yourself sufficient time to make the grade,—a minimum of ten years. It can take that long to break into the game even if you are both lucky and talented. Ten years may seem a long time to the young, but the very same brutal ten year baptism period is applicable elsewhere in many businesses and professions. It can easily take ten years for lawyers to make partner, ten for doctors and dentists to emerge into private practice, ten to find a mentor and survive in a corporate situation; ten or out is a fairly general rule of the time period necessary to become golden.

It helps to be financially independent or to have a wealthy indulgent parent, if you are going to make the movie business commitment. It can also help to be gay, by the way, as Mike Ovitz made more than clear in his recent VANITY FAIR soul-searching and—searing statement. And for some reason, which I have never understood, it helps to have no more than a high-school education, an addiction to the limelight and politics which are extreme left.

The ten years to survive is the first ten, followed by ten more to climb the ladder as far as you can, ten more to flourish as best you can, and ten to ride the backs of the newest crop of young ones. That is the crude norm for a career in American business anywhere.

The movie industry is in some respects different. The younger you are the better. It is more of a young persons' business than most other industries or professions. More than the case elsewhere, it is all relationships, and how well you play the politics. Network, network, network, and try, try and try again, the town gossips and revels in disaster, and never forgives the quitter, but ultimately forgives failure, at least for those with talent.

That is one of the best things about the place, the willingness to forgive failure. "He paid his dues" is the customary phrase, delivered with emotion.

The flip side of the same coin tends to be a bit ugly. In Europe, when a major talent has a flop, everyone says isn't that too bad and hopes he does better next time out. In Hollywood, when someone has a huge success, many people cannot wait for him to fall on his face so they can chortle and gossip that his agent won't take his phone calls. He can, however, come back once again and, if and when he does, all will be forgiven. That's Hollywood.

But you must live in Hollywood.

I discovered the importance of presence on the scene way back when, when I was a mysterious A-list, overeducated Boston lawyer, financially independent and derisive about most talent, including my own. I couldn't cut it in the life out there and kept fleeing east, 3,000 miles and then double that. I once walked off a picture and when they asked me why, I told them the truth. I missed my dog. I did miss him. He liked me. I could trust him.

Back on the other coast, I gradually became aware of something truly peculiar. There I was with two big hits, THE THOMAS CROWN AFFAIR and BULLITT, both earning net profits, and the phone never rang, even before the problem with Stan Kamen. Was it because I was too difficult? Too expensive? I supposed that was possible, being the highest paid screenwriter in the business.

Timidly, I started to make phone calls. Virtually no one took my calls. Only the fewest of the few of the calls were even returned. So I decided to beard the lions in their dens and went west for a week in Los Angeles, a suite at the Bel Air where I nearly went bankrupt with the phone call charges. Like all other Angelenos in the business, I was living on the telephone, and guess what? The very same people who would not call me back on the east coast now took my calls or called back promptly and invited me to meetings, screenings, breakfasts, lunches and even dinners. I was there, a member of the motion picture community—but the phone calls suddenly stopped, all at once, the very moment I went to the airport.

I have paid a heavy price for my inability to live in Los Angeles, but I truly don't like it there. I am not a people person and the need to network, network, network and sell, sell, sell is to me maddening. I can't stand sitting around endlessly, waiting for the phone to ring, taking useless meetings, feeling unproductive, fighting off the impulse to do something foolish, wondering why I am wasting my life, and so I don't live there.

That's one of my problems.
But only one of them.

21

SOME WHO HAVE GONE WEST AND MADE IT

I met Ed Zwick in the 1970's, in the spring of the year he graduated from Harvard or perhaps the Harvard Business School; it could have been either, I don't remember.

Ed came to my home for a bagel bakeoff, a party where everybody brought bagels from his favorite bakery so we could pick the best Boston bagel bakery. He told me he was going to be a director and I snickered and asked if he was prepared to spend the rest of his life in Los Angeles. Of course, he said. I said I hoped they didn't break his heart, and told him to give it a full ten years. He did, and more.

He directed and produced one episode of FAMILY in 1976 and seemed to disappear for the next six years. When I checked, I couldn't find out what he was doing. He reappeared in the early 1980's directing PAPER DOLLS and HAVING IT ALL for TV in 1982, and writing, directing and producing SPECIAL BULLETIN for TV the following year. He directed ABOUT LAST NIGHT…in 1986. Then came his big score, the TV series THIRTY SOMETHING which he wrote, directed and executive produced. He celebrated his ascendancy to financial independence and A-list status with GLORY, based on a fine script by my former dog-sitter, Kevin Jarre, who now hates me, but that is another story. GLORY is one of the best war movies ever made, and for me it answered a question puzzling me for half a century. Harvard's Memorial Hall plaques set forth the names of hundreds, possibly thousands, of alumni who died in the Civil War. Why were Civil War casualties so high? GLORY explained it in one memorable scene. Long dense lines of soldiers on each side faced each other a hundred yards apart and fired repeatedly, slaughtering those on the other side. Incredible, the carnage.

Since GLORY, Ed has directed LEAVING NORMAL, LEGENDS OF THE FALL, COURAGE UNDER FIRE and THE SIEGE, and has produced SHAKESPEARE IN LOVE, EXECUTIVE SEARCH, TRAFFIC, I AM SAM and last year's stinker, ABANDON. He will continue to be a factor in the industry unless he directs or produces a string of flops, and that is not going to happen; he is by far too talented and much, much too intelligent.

Roger Kumble is the son of my old friend, Steve Kumble, who revolutionized the practice of law, much to the benefit of lawyer incomes and definitely not to the benefit of their clients or the cost of access of people generally to our civil justice system. Roger dismayed his father by announcing on his graduation from college that he was going off to Hollywood to direct movies. Yeah, sure. He did go off to Hollywood and he did get to direct movies. It took him pretty much the usual ten full years. In the meantime, he did a bit of writing, and was very nicely paid for his work on DUMB AND DUMBER, KINGPIN, and THERE'S SOMETHING ABOUT MARY. He broke through with CRUEL INTENTIONS, which he wrote and directed in the year 2000, after which he shifted agents and was packaged into the ill-fated Cameron Diaz movie, THE SWEETEST THING. Roger is talented and will hopefully outgrow his current slot as a director of teenage comedies. We are waiting expectantly for his next pictures.

Doug Liman graduated from Brown in 1988. I ran into his widowed mother at a dinner party several years ago and she told me that Doug had moved to Los Angeles and based on talent shown at college, she was confident that he was going to be a successful director. I sympathized and told her to be patient, it would probably take 10 to 15 years, but at least he had the sense to relocate to Los Angeles, and that was especially wise in his case as his father was during his lifetime arguably the leading trial lawyer in the country, a tough act to follow in New York but somewhat easier 3,000 miles away where no one ever heard of Arthur Liman.

I started to follow what Doug was doing. At first, that wasn't much. I think he was going to one of the Los Angeles film schools. During the mid-1990's, he directed three teenage comedies, GETTING IN, SWINGERS and GO, each one more successful than the one before, but he seemed to be getting type-cast in that genre. He produced SEE JANE RUN and KISSING JESSICA STEIN last year, which did nothing to dispel my genre lock fears. Then he did THE BOURNE IDENTITY.

Once upon a time, I did a screenplay for THE OSTERMAN WEEKEND and read most of the Ludlums up to that time, enough of them to understand the reasons screen translations of the Ludlum novels are so difficult. The slender premises straining credulity, the endless mindless violence, the cold characters and the morbid fascination with the double double cross are not a recipe for screen success. I considered BOURNE IDENTITY hopeless and we had the Academy viewing cassette for three weeks before I could whip up the willingness to watch it.

It was terrific! Notwithstanding its soft opening and closing scenes, it maintains a constant level of high tension and grips audience attention from beginning to end. Matt Damon gives his best and most understated performance to date. He has arrived, has Doug Liman.

He is busy preparing a picture with Brad Pitt.

22

THE THIRD SOUL SEARCH

So much for recent success stories.

You still have to search your soul one more time, and this is the most difficult. Ask yourself how tough you are? How much patience do you have? And how stable are you?

Pinning your hopes, and career, on one screenplay, is not the prudent way to make the Hollywood grade. In diversity lies sanity.

Trying to market a single screenplay risks endless, heartbreaking waiting for return calls that never come, reads that never happen, the probability of negative coverage you will never see, and a series of cruel rejections.

Given the difficulty of getting a movie made, pretty much any movie, most of those who survive out there have based their careers and emotional stability on having multiple projects in the works all the time. When nothing is happening on one front, they can work on the others. When one project is rejected, they can try again with another.

Please pay attention to that lesson. Otherwise you may wake up one day with the feeling that you are playing postcard chess with a series of unreliable opponents, making a move, mailing the card, waiting for your opponent to write you back, and spending all the rest of your time thinking what moves you might make next if the opponent is willing to continue the play, and selling a movie is more awful than postcard chess because the opponents are always quitting, sometimes without bothering to mail you back that they have no interest and are quitting.

At least with multiple projects in play at one time, you pretty much always have something going on, and delay and rejection day after day are that much less devastating.

How many projects should you have?

I was lucky. I hit with my first two screenplays, thanks to one of the major agencies and a committed brilliant agent.

Since then, it has always been normal time and normal time is endless time. Hopefully, you are tougher than I am.

For me, the magic number has always been five. Unless I have five producible screenplays, I don't stick my toe in that ocean.

You may decide to try it one at a time or with several screenplays all at once. The remaining chapters of this book are applicable to each separate screenplay, the key word being "separate".

But—never submit more that one screenplay to one person at one time. The moment you even mention the existence of a second script, you will have killed both screenplays in one blow, and you may not know that you now have two dead scripts.

23

PLAN A:
THE GREEN-LIGHTER

Back to you once again.

Okay. You have canned your pitch expertly. You are prepared to proclaim your director and producer ambitions to everyone and sundry. You have moved yourself and your loved ones to Los Angeles for the ten years that may be necessary and you have somehow garnered from ancestors, family and friends the very necessary support money. You have worked the town for a couple of months and you do know some people, so it may be time to try to sell your screenplay. Or several screenplays, one at a time.

How do you go about it?

First, if you can, proceed to Plan A: Get access to a green-lighter. There is at least one person at every studio who has go-power, the authority to green-light a project. If you have access to such a person through a relative, friend, lover, agent, anyone, and you can get a personal meeting, take it (remember that "take" is Hollywoodese for attending a meeting) and deliver your pitch. You will know on the spot if the pitchee is inter-ested in your script.

If you are offered a meeting with anyone else, even if the offeree has an impressive title such as President or Senior Vice-President of something, don't take the meeting. If you do, you will get a polite five minutes and, if your pitch is sufficiently exciting so the pitchee asks for your script, it will in all likeli-hood go out for coverage, and the coverage will of course be negative, effectively killing your script. Further, if you play diffi-cult and refuse the meeting, there is a slight chance th' green-lighter will be sufficiently intrigued to c' personally anyhow, and if not, your refusal to r.

subordinate and the resulting irritation will not be fatal to your script.

They admire outrageous conduct throughout movie Los Angeles. Some of the time.

Item: Fred Weintraub loved the script for THE PACK but the other Warner Bros. executives didn't. He rented a trained German Shepherd attack dog, put the script in the dog's mouth and sent the animal into the New York conference room during the Tuesday morning meeting. The dog growled, cornered the executives, dropped the script in front of them and kept on growling until Fred entered the room and called him off. THE PACK was unanimously approved on the spot by the terrified executives present. No, the movie was not a success. Fred, still a joker, is active to this day, producing low-cost series abroad for U.S. cable television.

My one and only contact with a green-lighter occurred many years ago and illustrates my own ignorance and arrogance bordering on idiocy as well as the powers of people with go-power. Back in the days when I was still a star, an A-list screenwriter collecting net, if you can believe it, net profits on my only two movies, the phone was not exactly ringing off the wall, but I was too dumb to notice anything odd about that.

Then David Begelman recruited me as a client of his, and Freddy Fields', new agency, International Creative Management. David promptly made an appointment for me to see someone named Barry Diller at ABC. I didn't want to work in television, I told David. Yes, but Diller is into movies for televi-ion, he wants you to do a two-hour movie for one of his protégés, someone he named, but I had never heard of the man, and it won't hurt for you to meet Barry, he's very smart, he's more than a comer, he's already arrived, and you could use some friends in this town with your reputation. What reputation? Difficult, that was my reputation.

Diller was pleasant and gracious. He welcomed me instantly, without the customary softening up wait in the lobby. He said nice things about my movies, and told me he had a 23-year-old protégé whom he thought had huge talent. What had the protégé done? A great movie for TV called DUEL.

I went ballistic. I had read the short story in PLAYBOY and tried to buy the rights for a feature film. I had a great idea for a movie where you start sympathizing with the person who is being chased by the big black truck and end up rooting for the man in the truck to kill his prey in the car being chased. Someone in Hollywood had bought it out from under me and made that stupid TV movie! Now I was sitting in the room with him!

"No," I told him, "I won't work for your man, I don't think he has any talent. And if that's who you want me to work for, I don't want to work for you. As a matter of fact, I don't want to work in television."

I stormed out.

Barry had already phoned David when I reported in. David was philosophical. "Look, if that's the way you feel, that's it."

What he had decided and did not say was that that was it for me as a client. I had three more meetings with producers and directors but I never had another meeting with a studio or TV head, not one, and although I had five more movies made in the next five years, David collected his commission and negotiated one of my rewrite deals, but otherwise did nothing. I did the packaging needed to get the pictures made, without the remotest understanding of what I was doing. Plan B was what I was doing.

The story has an epilogue. In fact, two of them. Eight years later, when David was head of Columbia, and the Barry Diller protégé with no talent was making a shark movie in Martha's Vineyard, David phoned me out of the blue and said they needed a rewrite, bad, please cover the phone around the clock for the next couple of days, the director would be calling.

He never called.

Twenty years after that, when the director with no talent had reached the pinnacle of the profession, I ran into Barry outside the Southampton, NY Cinema, and recalled the long-ago session in his office. We had a good laugh together at my foolishness and bad judgment. Barry did the louder laughing.

Barry had been the green-lighter at ABC and although green-lighters normally decline responsibility for project selection by delegating project review to lower levels of development executives, most green-lighters will on a few occasions flex their muscles and take a chance. Rare ones like Barry Diller are not afraid to make their own decisions, their own project selections, and this is vastly more likely where they are trying to come up with a project for a protégé or favorite director, actor or producer, as Barry was when David Begelman sent me to him. I was too stupid to know the score. Barry rolled on to success after success and the director with no talent became the most successful director of his generation, and I paid the price for my foolishness at the unsuccessful meeting.

24

PLAN B: THE STAR ELEMENT

Back to you, and marketing your screenplay again: If you are unable to proceed with Plan A, or if you try and fail at Plan A, proceed to Plan B: Get access to a star element.

This is extraordinarily difficult, as such elements are as noted above treated as crown jewels. They are surrounded and access to them is closely guarded by staff, spouse, lover, agent and manager.

Do not expect to reach a star element through his agent. The standard approach to such a bid is eight weeks of silence followed by a "Make me a money offer or I won't let him read." The justification is protection of the agent from a situation where the star element loves a script—and the agent can't set up the project. From the point of view of the writer, however, this is one of the many industry Catch-22's. You need the star element to get your movie made and you can't get the star element even to hear about your script unless you have a financed package.

Offering to let the agent represent the entire package may work, but only sometimes.

Young hot directors with one box-office smash hit are among the hardest-to-reach star elements. In many cases, you will find that they have just shifted their representation to one of the three large agencies based on promises of big money and big packages with big stars. They want and may need the big money, and initial success in the business seems to whet the appetite for more success and make them highly vulnerable to flattery, promises and other forms of agent manipulation.

A director with one major success should be looking for something in which he really believes and which he feels will advance his career, even if it is a small picture. Many such directors are, however, easily seduced into agency-packaged two-year black holes of star actor self-indulgence, or their own self-indulgence. No matter how much money they are paid, and how big the budgets of the pictures to which they commit, it will never, or almost never, be worth it. It can take years to recover from one huge career disaster.

Okay, you need a personal meeting with a star element so you have a chance to deliver your well-rehearsed pitch. You can get the personal meeting through a relative, friend, lover or agent, or again, by doing something outrageous. Please be forewarned: your script is going, almost certainly, to be sent out for coverage unless your pitch delivery is so successful that you can ask the pitchee to read the script himself ASAP and not send it out for coverage because if he wants to pass, you are going to take it to another bankable element and you do not want the customary negative coverage circulating anywhere in this town. If your pitch is not that successful, in most cases you will know it because the star pitchee will tell you that he is going to be discussing the matter with his agent, manager, personal assistant, partner or someone else in his organization, and if that happens you should seriously consider walking out without leaving your script behind and refusing to forward your script even if they ask for it then or later because, unless there is some sort of miracle, your Plan B approach to that star will be dead, dead, dead, and you should be smart enough to know it.

On the other hand, you cannot overestimate the power of star elements in the current environment. Star elements are the key to securing financing in advance of production and the key to favorable distribution and other exploitation deals when the picture is nearly complete and the studio marketing department is desperately trying to create the buzz needed for the deals and the marketing blitz. Star elements are so important that they have power and influence beyond the particular projects for which they are the key to exploitation. They are sometimes so powerful that they can, in effect, make any movie they want.

A good case in point was the remake of my THE THOMAS CROWN AFFAIR. Do you think MGM/UA remade the movie because it was a style classic, or because they expected to do huge business, or because remakes were all the fashion the year the "go" decision was made? Wrong, no way, all wrong. MGM/UA had to remake it because Pierce Brosnan had always loved the original movie, and he wanted to remake it with himself starring in the Steve McQueen role,—and Pierce Brosnan is the current James Bond. James Bond is the one of the most, if not the most, valuable MGM/UA franchise. Each new James Bond does huge business. Each new James Bond makes huge profits. Audiences have gotten used to Pierce Brosnan as James bond and they are unlikely to accept anyone else with the possible exception of Sean Connery, who is unwilling to play the role any more. As a result, Pierce Brosnan could probably persuade MGM/UA to make a movie out of the Los Angeles phone book if he wished. They would make it, release it, and bury it, considering it as a necessary cost of the next James Bond. Pierce Brosnan could get your movie made at MGM/UA, if only you could get to him.

Another illustration of star power was MOTORDRONE, a feature about motorcycle racing in indoor arenas. It was rejected by seven studios when it was submitted as a naked script, and then approved a month later with Steve McQueen attached by the very same seven studios. The competitive bidding was under way when it was discovered much to everyone's shock that Steve was ill and dying.

25

PLAN C:
GET AN AGENT

Every book I have ever seen about how to sell a screenplay or how to make it in the business, starts off by telling you to get an agent. Clearly I started off in the business because I was lucky enough to get an agent.

But here we are in Chapter Twenty-Five and only now am I suggesting that if you can't get access to a greenlighter, and if you can't get a star element, your next choice is Plan C: get an agent.

Why?

Because this may be the hardest sell of all. There are numerous small agencies that do very good work representing established screenwriters, and some of them have succeeded at getting high prices for first-time screenwriter speculative scripts. The odds against a small agency doing that for you are, unfortunately, very high. A newcomer has the greatest chance if he can obtain representation from one of the three major talent agencies, William Morris, International Creative Management or Creative Artists Agency.

All three of the major agencies, however, already represent dozens of screenwriters, are having difficulty finding work for most of them and are agonizing over the difficulty holding onto those screenwriters who have achieved success. The last thing they need is an additional unproven writer.

If you are over 40, by the way, you may not be able to get an agent. This is one of several areas in the industry where ageism is rampant. It is not the fault of the agents. Who would want to represent a writer when you cannot take him to pitch meetings? Most studio and other pitchee types are in their early 30's or younger and painfully lacking in movie experience; they are uncomfortable, to say the least, meeting with writers older than 40, particularly writers with movie experience. When I was on the Negotiating Committee for the Writers Guild at the time of the 1987 strike, we were advised that white Anglo-Saxon males over 40 were legally a protected class under the anti-discrimination laws of both California and the United States, and there were several such writers present at our meetings, but neither they, nor the Committee, nor the Guild nor anyone else was willing to tilt at that windmill in the California or federal courts. Recently some distinguished television writers have been trying, hard, with singular lack of success thus far. For details, take a look at www.writerscase.com.

Assuming you are age-appropriate and properly prepared with samples of your writing, you may be able to get a meeting with an agent. If it is a meeting with one of the major agencies, you absolutely must bear in mind what they want and tailor your pitch accordingly. What do they want? The large agencies will not be primarily interested in selling your script for lots of money. No, what they really want is a package where they represent a number of elements.

When you pitch to a major agency, bear in mind whom else they represent, and don't worry about the conflict of interest if they represent both you and a star actor or director. You want—need—a package so that your movie gets made, and you will be paid significantly more, not less, if a star actor or director wants to commit to your project. Always assume that if you are successful in your agent pitch, the pitchee will want to represent the project and try to package the entire project instead of just trying to sell your script.

Chapter Twelve has made clear the power of agents, and what you can expect from them. The unexpected can be a more serious problem and agents can be as imaginative, perverse, destructive and crazy as anyone else in this wonderful industry. Case in point: my David Begelman.

After I blew the meeting with Barry Diller, David cleverly set up three more meetings with Famous People, one producer and two directors. I found myself in the presence of powerhouse egomaniacs, two of whom had red eyes and traces of white powder below their noses, and neither I nor those two, nor the third, an industry icon, had any idea of what we were talking about. My attempts to direct the conversation to the matters David had specified as the purpose of the meetings and my desperate suggestions of other subject matter I wanted to write about were instantly brushed off with brusque impatience. It is possible that David had agreed with them in advance on what we were going to discuss and they had simply forgotten, or were substance-induced unable to recall, but whatever the mental or emotional problems on the other side of the desks, it was clear that they had no interest whatsoever in pretty much anything I had to say and my attempts to direct the conversations in any direction were received as irritating.

In the two cases of substance abuse, they went off into a series of raves about matters that had nothing whatsoever to do with me, or David, or whatever they had been talking about in the immediately preceding sentence. It was my first experience with the white powder and I extricated myself from those meetings feeling foolish and from the third meeting feeling crushed as I really admired the man and wanted to work with him.

In retrospect, it seems to me that David knew what he was doing. It was payback for the Diller fiasco and next David ratcheted up from there to something deft, crushing and brilliant.

One day David phoned me and announced with huge excitement a glorious five-picture deal for me with Richard Zanuck and David Brown, at the time the Twentieth Century Fox management. I had a blank check on subject matter, one screenplay a year, they got a first look, and I was to be paid half a million dollars per, against five percent of the gross if it were made, with a "turnaround" right to take each project elsewhere if they passed on it.

It was a spectacular deal for a screenwriter, the best I had ever heard about, and even Bob Montgomery was impressed. Bob was my lawyer, a lovely man, an old friend, probably the preeminent movie lawyer in New York, and head of the entertainment department at Paul, Weiss, Rifkind. Bob and David entered into heavy negotiations with Fox over what was meant by "gross". Was it studio gross, as David had said, or producer gross, which I indignantly refused, or some sort of compromise on studio gross with an array of deductions?

The negotiations went on and on with David phoning Bob several times a week and phoning me excitedly every day, including Saturdays and Sundays, every single day, to report on the latest negotiation twists and turns, and to set up the necessary conference calls with Bob to agree on what we would propose next. David, who had made the deal in the first place, and was an acknowledged master negotiator, was our point man in the negotiations. After seven weeks without a conclusion, however, I woke up with a paranoid seizure at 2:00 am one morning.

Bob was an early riser so I phoned him at home at 8:00 am, coffee time. "Don't worry," Bob assured me, "movie negotiations can go on for years, and there have even been situations where the picture is actually released while the lawyers are still arguing."

"Your situations?"

"Well, no, but I have certainly heard of some. And listen, David is the best, and no one is going to welsh on him."

"Bob, do you know Zanuck or Brown?"

Pause. "You want me to phone them? He hesitated again and went on, "I couldn't do that to David, he would resent my going around him."

"Bob, Zanuck and Brown have agreed to pay me half a million a year for five years, and this has been going on for weeks now, and I have never met them."

"What are you suggesting? David can't be making it up. David is a busy man. The time he has spent on the phone with me—"

"With me, too. Every day. You must know someone down the line at Fox, a secretary, an assistant."

Bob sighed. "I'll call you after lunch."

He did. He was laughing. "There are lots of Begelman stories," he said, "but this one tops all of them. No one at Fox ever heard of your deal. Not Zanuck, not Brown, no one. And please, never ask me how I found out."

"What's your advice? Call David on the fraud?"

"Let it go."

"Don't do a thing?"

"No. No, David can hurt you if he wants. Better to do nothing."

That's what I did, nothing. David continued to phone me for another five weeks and conference-called Bob in on three of the conversations, but gradually his telephone calls petered out.

He and I never discussed Zanuck, Brown, Fox or the deal even once, ever again.

What is the lesson to be learned from this? Lying in the business is an art form and please remember always that the other person may be lying, even if there is no reason to lie other than practice in the art of lying.

Onward, and sideways if not upward.

I should have gone to a producer then and I would have if I had thought of it or understood the business.

Unfortunately, I didn't.

26

PLAN D:
LURE A PRODUCER IN

Okay. You can't a green-lighter to green-light your script. You can't get an A-list element and you can't get an agent.

What do you try to do next?

Plan D: Get a producer. After all, that's what producers do. They get the pictures made. They do the packaging.

At any given time there are a half dozen red hot producers who can get anything made into a movie if that is what they want. One or two of them will be nice people and the rest will be monsters.

But they have all mastered the packaging art and they all have universal access. Studio executives and director and actor stars will all take their phone calls. They are always in production on something and frequently in production on several movies at the same time and they always have their next half dozen projects in gestation. They will all be receptive to a really good pitch,—if you can get the personal meeting needed to deliver a good one-on-one pitch.

They all have ongoing relationships with lots of favorite writers, so do not under any circumstances option your screenplay to a producer. It is a sure way to find yourself out of your own project. On the other hand, they have access to studio and investor funding as well as their own and they can make an instant buy of a script. Further, you can go to one of the major agencies and ask them to negotiate your deal for you if a producer wants to buy your script, and that is probably the most effective way for an outsider to get an agent.

How do you get a producer to read your script?

One technique was taught to students in the UCLA Film School course in producing. You pretend to be a messenger and leave your script for producers A, B, C and D, mentioning to each of their receptionists as you are leaving that the script is being read by the other three, in fact it is on their desks at the very moment.

Another possibility, and a good one: get yourself a movie lawyer. Movie lawyers are more than lawyers. They are conduits to major players. They know lots of the key people and represent talent, studio executives and producers. If they like what you have written, they can introduce you to them. Accordingly some lawyers will read scripts. They have to before leading you to anyone else. They cannot afford to be embarrassed with their clients. They will have to tell whoever it is that they have read it, and liked it, and think it is commercial, and this is particularly true when talking to their producer clients.

Back to me, and my two Begelman fiascoes. David was one of the very best agents there was, brilliant and knowledgeable, if quirky and unstable. There was no point in going to anyone else. What to do? Give up on the business? Quit? Seek out producers on my own?

I decided to package my scripts myself. I would find the actors and directors myself, and get the studios to fund my deals and then sell my screenplays to them, refusing to talk money; I would let David do the negotiations.

So I became a producer myself, without understanding that I was producing.

27

PRODUCER ADVENTURES: THEY CALL ME MR. TIBBS

Decision made, I was going to produce myself.

I no sooner decided to go that way than I was promptly detoured by an unexpected blast from the past. Walter Mirisch phoned. He had activated THEY CALL ME MR. TIBBS, a script I had written two years earlier in response to his challenge, "Do you think you can do an original sequel to IN THE HEAT OF THE NIGHT without Rod Steiger?" I wrote it and it wasn't half bad. It was, however, before the day of the Blacksploitation movies and I had made Tibbs a hardass homicide cop in Philadelphia, a bit ahead of its time for Hollywood, and something quite new for Sidney Poitier.

"When I walk down the streets of New York," Sidney told me, "people turn and they look at me and they smile. Do you know why they smile?"

"Why is that?" I responded on cue.

"Because I radiate all that fucking goodness."

"Oh."

"Now you make me radiate all that fucking goodness or I won't do your movie."

I didn't, and he didn't.

But times had changed, and now he would. Delighted, I flew to LAX, where a terrible thing happened. There was no limousine and driver waiting at the airport to meet me.

Nothing of the kind had ever happened to me in Hollywood before. I considered taking the next plane east back home.

Instead, I took a taxi.

At the Beverly Hills Hotel, another terrible thing happened. I did not get my usual bungalow. Instead, some idiot had reserved a room. Can you imagine? A room. Not even a suite. I was a star! Or was I? I moved to a suite at my own expense.

Bright and early the following day, I showed up at the Goldwyn Studio, where Walter greeted me effusively and told me he was occupied on another picture and had hired someone else to line produce my TIBBS. He apologized for the no-limo and no-suite, he would pay all my expenses, and alert the line producer to my status as a friend. Could I please come back after lunch to meet the man?

I spent the morning prowling the lot and greeting old friends from THE THOMAS CROWN AFFAIR crew, and a few other non-friends I had done favors for in Boston. I had lunch in the commissary and there the atmosphere felt a bit strange. Curious. What was happening?

After lunch I had the meeting with the line producer, whose name I have suppressed, and the director he had chosen, who told me in the first five minutes that Norman Jewison had no talent. Norman had been very nice to me. He had come to see me in Boston and taught me how to write in the screenplay form. It had been a pleasure working with him and I thought him a major talent. What the hell. I said nothing.

They gave me three pages of written "notes". No one had ever given me notes before and I wasn't quite sure what to make of them. Clearly they were comments. Pretty clearly they were suggestions. Possibly they were demands as well although, as a star, I might find demands demeaning. Again, what the hell. I would consider, rewrite, and see them in the morning.

That appeared to startle them. I could have more time if I wanted it. Thank you but I wouldn't need it, they would see me in the morning.

I did the rewrite back at the hotel that afternoon and evening. I made all of the changes they had asked, including both of the stupid ones, and showed up on the lot at the appointed 9:00 am. They were late. I fidgeted. 10:00 am? 11:00? Enough. I phoned Walter. He was off the lot. His secretary, Jessie, a kind and motherly woman, volunteered to track the missing line producer and director down, and she did. They were sorry, they said, they had left a message for me at the hotel, they would see me on the lot at 3:00 pm, they were off scouting locations.

I decided not to fume, and prowled the lot, saying a few more hello's again, and had lunch at the commissary, where a strange thing happened. No one sat at the table with me, and one friend head-gestured to see him outside. He was waiting in the shadows across the way and handed me a list. People's names, a dozen of them. All unfamiliar. I knew none of the names. "Who are they?" I asked.

"No comment," he said, "and forget you got the list from me." He walked off.

I showed up on time for the 3:00 pm and contemplated the list until 5:30 pm. The line producer and director never phoned or showed. As I was approaching my rental car to leave the lot, Jessie was also leaving. I showed her the list. "What's this?" she said.

"Do you know these people?" I said.

"Some of them. They're writers. Why?"

"That's what I thought."

"Oh, my God," she said. "Look, you never showed that list to me. Okay?"

"Sure."

She looked worried as I was leaving.

Back at the hotel, and two martinis later, I decided to phone Walter at his home.

"Hi, what's up?" he said, cheerful enough.

"I just called to say good-bye," I said.

"Oh oh. What happened?"

"They asked for a rewrite, which was fine, and I did it, all the things they asked, but they stood me up on the lot twice today and let me know, possibly deliberately, that they don't have the slightest interest in anything I have written."

"I don't understand. How did they let you know?"

"There's a list of the other writers they plan to hire the moment I am gone. Writers who are friends of theirs. I never heard of them and don't know them."

"There couldn't possibly be such a list—"

"There is, Walter. I have it."

"Jesus," he said. Walter is not a swearing man. "I don't suppose you want to tell me how you got the list?"

"I do want to tell you," I said, "but I can't, I seem to have forgotten. Walter, this is now him or me. He goes or I go, and he's been preparing this for weeks. He has the director, of that I'm sure. By the way, the director told me that Norman has no talent."

Walter laughed. "You're kidding."

"It all comes down to Sidney and they must have been working on him," I said. "U.A. only cares about Sidney."

"That's not true," Walter said. "Arthur Krim and David Picker love you, and your doing the rewrites was a factor in their go decision. Stick around for another day or two."

"And what? You'll see what you can do? It's a loser, Walter. You know it is."

"Please stick around for another day or two."

I spent two days at the Beverly Hills Hotel swimming pool, a true heaven for crazy people watching, and then Walter phoned. He was sorry, he really tried hard, but. He would pick up all my expenses, of course, he should have anticipated something like this and he was sorry, but he didn't.

Walter is a gentleman and I believe him.

I took the red-eye east later on the second evening.

Actually, the movie wasn't half bad and despite the hard edge of my script, Sidney did manage to radiate all that fucking goodness on the screen.

A fine actor, Sidney, one of the best. I have always admired him.

28

PRODUCER ADVENTURES: LADY ICE

I went off to play packager-producer without understanding what I was doing.

It was the worst three years I have ever had. I went after actors, which was a bad mistake. I should have lassoed directors first. Chalk the error up to innocence and lack of information.

It wasn't all bad times and some of it was fun and games, cycling from Boston to New York to Los Angeles to New York, to London, to Paris and Rome and back again, pitching, pitching.

I was no longer a star in Los Angeles but elsewhere I had a fine reputation so it was easy to get the meetings. I was flush and enjoyed the first class on the planes, the suites at the Bel Air in Beverly Hills, the New York Sherry Netherlands, the London Connaught, the Paris Ritz, the Hassler in Rome, and I was married to a woman who enjoyed the life, especially the shopping, especially in London. In London, we carried no money. "Deliver it to the Hall Porter at the Connaught," we said, and they did, and presented the bill, and the Hall Porter paid the bill and called my London bank for reimbursement.

London was very heady stuff, drinks with Micky Caine at his club, Sean Connery lifting my wife by the elbows out of his way when she was blocking his exit in the aisle after a preview screening, dinner with Albie Finney and Anouk Aimee at their flat. Notice the self-important use of the nicknames. Cocktails and hors d'oeuvres with Karel Reisz at his home and a lecture on the fine points of editing. Rome was Suso Cecchi D'Amico, of whom you have never heard, despite her hundreds of writing credits, her friendship with Fellini, Antonioni and Visconti, to all of whom she introduced me, and Mastroianni whom Suso mothered either in person or on the phone every day even when he was working in Moscow and dependent on the Russian telephone system. Valentina Cortesa after DAY FOR NIGHT, and would I like to meet with Francois Truffaut? All of which was heady stuff for an over-his-head boy from Boston.

I got Donald Sutherland and Susan George, then Jennifer O'Neill, Robert Duvall and Patrick Magee for LADY ICE, Richard Pryor and Billy Dee Williams for HIT!, Omar Sharif and Karen Black for CRIME AND PASSION and Sean Connery for THE NEXT MAN. Sounds wonderful, doesn't it?

The realities were very different. It was painful and an education.

I needed someone to line produce LADY ICE and Bob Montgomery introduced me to Harrison Starr. It was love at first sight, for me, anyhow, a magical introduction. Harrison was exactly what I was looking for. He came to visit me in my home for a couple of weeks to discuss the situation.

Fish and guests stink in three days, two if you are like me and don't like people in your home, but Harrison didn't stink. Pepper did. Harrison brought Pepper with him. Pepper was a red setter of some kind, frisky with personality, and keeping him safe from my two German Shepherds was a chore, particularly when Harrison was gone from the house to his dojo or whatever you call the place he went daily to do his judo thing, but Harrison and I were having a wonderful time.

That lasted until Harrison fed Pepper his dinner one night out of one of my wife-at-the-time's favorite large French copper frying pans, and she delivered herself of the memorable line: "Harrison, if you feed that dog out of my frying pan again, I WILL hit you over the head with it and I don't care if you leave me!"

Harrison had the grace to laugh. I didn't.

We took the LADY ICE script to United Artists. They loved the script but called me privately and objected to working with Harrison. I was adamant. I needed him. We made the deal. The papers were signed. We were paid. UA had asked for talent approval rights and we granted that to them.

Mistake.

They turned down our actor suggestions and six, count 'em, six director choices, including Claude Chabrol of whom they had never heard, they said, and Bernardo Bertolucci, of whom they had never heard, they said, even after THE CONFORM-IST. Not two years later, they hired Bertolucci for the LAST TANGO IN PARIS, on which he demonstrated, according to his many friends and admirers in Rome, a degree of writer and director flexibility that can only be described as sheer genius. When Brando became uncontrollable and repeatedly refused to shoot the script, Bertrolucci let the famous actor do whatever he wished and cut the shot film into what was largely a documentary about the inner sexual torments of his actor subject. A great movie if not much of a box office success.

Weary of having our director choices rejected, we moved our LADY ICE project to the Tomorrow Entertainment division of General Electric for their one and only venture into feature films. We refused to assume responsibility for budget overruns and gave them the unconditional right to take the production over if they wished themselves. We signed the contract on my birthday and they paid United Artists out. On the following day, they refused our director choice. I flew the man from London to Los Angeles at my own expense and they canceled two meetings with him and finally talked to him in a limousine between two appointments. They again refused to approve him.

We were stunned but there was more to come. Eight days later on Christmas day, they moved the production office from New York to Los Angeles and hired four production executives we had never heard of, without any discussion.

Obviously they had taken control. Would I have signed if I had known what would happen? No, but I had signed the agreement. I would honor my commitment. Under the contract, if they took control, I had no further responsibilities and no further function, so I quit.

I gave them one piece of advice in leaving. I suggested they pay Harrison off and told them that otherwise Harrison would eat their people alive. He was much stronger than all four of their men combined and vastly more experienced. He would finish the picture no matter what they did but they would find it hell working with him. Tomorrow Entertainment decided to keep Harrison on.

I had no further contact with them for a time, except for occasional phone conversations with Harrison who told me of their problems.

Eight months, two directors, two leading ladies, six intervening writers and four production executives later, Tomorrow Entertainment phoned me. They were way over budget. Would I please help them?

Of course I would. I flew to Miami, and asked what was wrong. Harrison told me to see Bob Swink, a fine editor and a good man, who had cut a lot of the shot film. What was the problem? Swink laughed. Look at the cut film.

I did, and understood the problem. Donald Sutherland wouldn't shoot the script and apparently no one could make him. He was having a wonderful time making it up as he went along, daily improvising. What was the point in rewriting the script if Donald wouldn't shoot it as written and kept on improvising?

That wasn't my job, that was theirs, wasn't it, controlling Donald Sutherland?

Harrison met me in the production office and introduced me to Tim, son of Fred, Zinneman. Tim was assistant director on the film and Harrison thought a lot of him. He was very smart and I liked him.

"This thing may be unreleasable," he said.

"Beg pardon?" I had never heard the word before. "Explain, please. What does that mean?"

"You don't know?"

"No. They'll release it, they have to," I said. "It is costing five million."

"Some movies are so bad they are not released," Tim explained. "Or they don't know how to sell them. So they never play in the theatres at all. They just sit there, with the answer print."

"And eat the five million?"

"Yes."

That was awful. No one had ever lost any money on me, let alone five million.

I had dinner with Donald Sutherland, a long, slow, mildly drunken meal, and gradually saw the solution to that part of the problem. I explained it to Harrison. Tell Donald to shoot the script or else he might have a really bad accident and find himself in the hospital with his arms and legs broken. I had friends available locally, as a matter of fact, people working for me, who could take care of the situation.

Harrison laughed. Why did I think he asked me to come to town?

Because of whom I knew?

Yes.

As for the rest of the problem, he wanted me to write a mostly new script that would make sense of the cut footage they had in the can. All right, I said I would do it, if Harrison was willing to promise me that Donald would shoot the new script and cease improvising.

Harrison promised to control Donald Sutherland.

I flew home and phoned David Begelman. Yes, they had been mean to me but they did have a big problem, please don't kill them on the money terms.

David blew up at me. "You know what? You don't belong in this business!" he snarled. "You want people to love you but no one in this business ever will! You want to make them love you by giving away your money, ten percent of which is my money! Not only will they not love you, they will have nothing but contempt for you!".

I told David to negotiate whatever deal he wished.

Wow! Did he ever! He got me $10,000 a week for four weeks—in 1973 dollars, by the way—with the understanding that I could remain in Massachusetts where I was then living and fax them three pages a day, five days a week. At the end of the fourth week, they wanted more, and David got me a two week extension, another $20,000.

I told you he was brilliant.

Shortly thereafter, Tomorrow Entertainment fired all four of their original hires and left it to Harrison to finish the film. He did, notwithstanding everything that had happened. The picture went over budget, and was barely the right side of unreleasable. I have always wondered what would have happened if they had made the movie we wanted from the script I had originally written, which bore little resemblance to the movie that was made, but so it goes, as Kurt Vonnegut says.

Tomorrow Entertainment made no more films and General Electric promptly liquidated Tomorrow Entertainment.

Harrison left the movie business for good. He went into real estate, at which he has done very well, and he has been married to the same woman for 33 years.

Congratulations to them!

29

PRODUCER ADVENTURES: HIT!

HIT! was the hottest game in town for ten days, with four studios loving it and going to bid,—only somehow they didn't.

I phoned Sidney J. Furie, the director to be. "Didn't you have someone named Korshak working for you on LADY SINGS THE BLUES?"

He did.

"Is he related to THE Korshak?"

He was.

"How?"

"Harry is Sidney's son."

"Well, Harry is now the producer. He's in and I'm out, I'm just selling the screenplay."

"What? Why?"

"You figure it out."

He did. At 11:00 o'clock the following morning, we closed a financing and distribution deal at Paramount.

Clever, huh?

That was. Our next step wasn't. We requested Charlie Bronson. Our script was about a man who loses his wife and child to heroin and recruits a small group to go to Marseilles and kill the major dealers. Bronson thought it was a great idea. So did Paramount.

But our project went into full stall.

Four months later we were told that Paramount was putting Bronson in something they were working on that had a plot that was similar.

Two months after that, we got the green light to make our movie with a black cast. Sidney Furie snapped up Billy Dee

Williams and Richard Pryor. I wasn't there while they shot the picture and the next thing I knew, they had run out of money and were forced to change the ending and eliminate most of my wonderful heroin dealer assassinations.

Nevertheless, the movie previewed in Times Square and rated 95% good or excellent. Paramount was enthusiastic. They projected domestic box office of $40 million, ten times the negative cost $4 million. I owned 26% of net profits. But I hated the picture, particularly the non-ending.

I offered to sell Paramount my interest and they agreed to buy me out for $1.5 million. Agreed over the phone, that is. When the papers were not forthcoming, I phoned a week later. They dropped the price to $1 million. I agreed again and flew to Los Angeles to close the deal. While I was waiting for the papers, in vain, I screened all the ending rushes and came up with an idea for a new ending assembled from the film they had shot. I offered to recut at my own expense. They refused and the price to buy me out was now $500,000. I agreed on condition they not offer me less. They agreed to the condition. They just never did the papers.

The movie did $800,000 domestic gross.

Sic transit my net profit participation.

DEATH WISH with Charlie Bronson and its numerous sequels all grossed many millions.

30

PRODUCER ADVENTURES: CRIME AND PASSION

CRIME AND PASSION was going to be line-produced by my old friend and former genius agent John Flaxman and directed by his good friend Teddy Flicker.

They arranged the financing and I sold them the screenplay. Notice how as time went on I was doing a good part of the packaging and then selling the screenplay instead of claiming a producer position.

If I had insisted on being a producer, I might very well have killed somebody on this one.

Flaxman and his wife and Flicker and his wife moved to Austria for the summer and prepared to shoot the picture. On the first day of principal photography, however, the people putting up the money fired them both and took over the production themselves. Wham, bam!

The new producer was the actor who drove the car in BULLITT chased by Steve McQueen's Mustang.

Flaxman was disgusted and so was I.

I heard nothing further until the picture was about to open at long last, of all places in Boston. I received a phone call from my old friend, law school classmate and former client Alan Friedberg at Sack Theatres. "Say, didn't you once tell me that you wrote CRIME AND PASSION?"

"Yes, why?"

"Well, we have the posters, and you get no writing credit."

"That's impossible," I said.

"Impossible, but true. Now what?"

Good question. Now what? What was I phoned the Writers Guild. I told them the story and they were shocked. They would look into it at once, and they did. They called me back the next day. Cautiously. "What about the arbitration?"

"What arbitration?" I said.

"The English arbitration."

"What English arbitration? And why England? It was shot in Austria."

"The other writers were English so there was an English arbitration. And you must have been notified of the English arbitration."

"No way," I told them. "I never received any notice of any arbitration. Ask the English Guild or whatever they are called how and when they claim they notified me of their arbitration."

They would.

They phoned again the following day. "You're not going to believe this."

"What?"

"Under the rules of the English guild," they said, "non-English writers not living in England do not have to be notified of an English arbitration."

I laughed.

"You find it amusing?"

"Yes," I said. "Could you please write me confirming all this and put the matter on the agenda for your next meeting with them."

They wrote me as requested.

I got a lawyer and sued to enjoin the picture opening. Not only did they fail to give me the credit, but the picture was shot in Austria where the law incorporates the French droit morale under which you can't change a word of a writer's work without his written permission.

The distributor offered me money and I refused. They offered me more and I still refused although the second offer was substantial, more than $50,000. There was an important principle at stake, I said, and besides I was angry with them for firing Flicker and Flaxman. I asked to see a screening and Alan Friedberg arranged the screening.

I hated the movie.

I hated it so much that if my name had appeared on it I would have sued to take my name off of it, or get a pseudonym credit or something.

I dropped the suit and paid my lawyer, who was angry with me.

The movie bombed when it opened.

31

PRODUCER ADVENTURES: THE NEXT MAN

THE NEXT MAN was a favor to Marty Bregman, who was courting Cornelia Sharp and had promised her a movie. Marty had a management company and ambitions to be a producer. He was intelligent, ambitious, determined, energetic, personable and I was impressed and fond of him and, for several years, I even financed his operation.

My contributions to management were exactly three. The first two were fiascos.

I believed in watching where my money went and noticed a thousand dollar payment to Dunhill the Tailor for a double-breasted suit. Oh oh. But it wasn't for Marty, I was relieved to find. It was for an actor client, and I questioned it. Marty's explanation was anything but satisfactory. The client was a short character actor who needed the suit to try out for the second lead in a forthcoming Coppola gangster film where he would play opposite Marlon Brando. I was furious. I was also wrong.

The client got the role and became a leading man.

My second intervention was similar. We represented an overweight girl singer from Hawaii with a loud voice and problems with impulse control and hired a superaggressive to manage her. He wanted to put her in a movie. What made him think the woman could act? What did he know about movies? Next thing I knew, he hired a director who had done the only slow movie Steve McQueen ever made, and got the project packaged. Incredible.

What was more incredible was how wrong I had been once again. I saw the movie five times. It is my all-time favorite spoof of the music scene and the lady was not only an actress, she was a brilliant comedienne who would be wasting her time if she kept singing. The superaggressive became a successful producer in his own right, and I never again tried to intervene in management.

I did, however, recruit Sidney Lumet for SERPICO, meeting him in the lobby of the Sherry Netherlands when he was down and nearly out, and regarded as unbankable despite his enormous talent. "How would you like to direct a cop movie, a major feature with Al Pacino?" I said. He thought it was a practical joke.

It wasn't, and he did two Al Pacino's, the second one the concept of Marty Elfand, loveable, gregarious, and out of his mind when he decided there was a movie in a ridiculous news item about a gay bank robber holding hostages in a bank. I thought it was a simply awful idea and would cost us the relationships with both Lumet and Pacino.

I was wrong again; it didn't.

As for THE NEXT MAN, I had nothing whatsoever to do with it after delivering the screenplay. I went back to being a writer, where I belonged, and a writer at a distance. I would hug the east coast from then on. My people skills, patience and tolerance for the unstable being markedly deficient, I was clearly not meant for the Hollywood scene. I would become invisible. I would ghost-write, use pseudonyms and refuse to do more than one rewrite even on my originals, and would make my money somewhere else. Packaging and producing were not for me.

I saw THE NEXT MAN and liked it and the project had the happiest possible ending: Marty Bregman married Cornelia Sharp and I hear they are happy right up to this day, one of the rare successful Hollywood marriages. Celebrity and the ability to sustain a marriage must be emotionally inconsistent.

A contented Marty Bregman went on to become one of the most active and successful producers of all time, with one or two features nearly every year from 1976 to the present, SCARFACE, SEA OF LOVE and CARLITO'S WAY being my favorites among his best ones.

Good things do come out of movies.

Some movies. Sometimes.

32

PLAN E: GET THEE AN ANGEL

No greenlighter, bankable element, agent or producer? Onward and downward.

Time for Plan E.

Get a commitment for partial financing from someone outside the business, someone who has the money and ought to know better and for some reason doesn't.

The wonderful world in which we live has an inexhaustible supply of assholes who love money, pursue it and live their lives for money and what it represents to them, a ticket to glamour, and celebrity, and girls. In many cases, primarily the girls. Every few years some of the richest of the rich turn up and dump millions of dollars, hundreds of millions of dollars, into the Hollywood bottomless pit.

The industry welcomes them with open arms. Pockets. Smiles. Whatever they want. Hollywood is just what you think it is, the home and happy hunting grounds of the world's most accomplished wizards in every form of seduction.

The place to look for the money is the current crop of zillionaires. For a while, it was the real estate tycoons, energized by their freakish low taxes. Then it was the Japanese, who bit, and dropped billions. Then it was the dot-com millionaires who made their money so quickly they were looking for ways to drop it.

Currently you are looking for Russians or the rare dot-com survivors.

They are out there and you can find them.

Lure them out to Hollywood, bring them to the major agencies, along with your pitch and script, and ask the agency to represent the package.

All of the major studios today are interested in finding outsiders to share the risk on most productions. As for the agencies, if you have half the production funds, that will be much more attractive to the studios and therefore to the agencies than your lonely naked pitch and script.

Raise as much money as possible, but never, never, offer to provide more than half the budget. You want the studio to have as much as possible of its own money in the project. If you provide more than $5 million and the studio less than $5 million for a $10 million negative cost picture, and the studio has $60 million of its own money invested in a stinker, which picture will get the best play dates and the largest budget for advertising?

Do not permit your angel to contribute to the print and advertising budget as the studio will control disbursement and from your angel's point of view the investment will be a bad one. For those who have tried it, it has been. If the picture is good, the studio will flog it for all it is worth at their own expense for the 15% to 30% distribution fee they will insist on clipping off the top, and if the picture is a bomb, your print and advertising money will somehow disappear and you will be told by the studio, "What could we do? The theatres canceled your booking."

Do not ever make the movie at your angel's expense and then take the finished film to the studios and ask them to distribute it. Your screening for the studio marketing executives will be the coldest, most humiliating experience of your life, even if some of them sit through the whole thing. They are trained to hate everything, and they do hate most everything. They will pretend to hate your picture even if they see something in it. Life is too short to spend two years of it pouring your heart and soul and your angel's money into a piece of film and then subjecting you and him to a screening for studio marketing executives.

A word of warning: your outside investor will probably lose his shirt, and if he is the sort of person who will blame you for losing his money, you are gambling the relationship and possibly more and the odds are heavily against you. That may well be the reason that the Russians have been teased and have occasionally bit but, to my knowledge to this day no one has as yet dared—or managed—to sucker the Russians into the business.

Apart from considerations of personal safety, however, you are going into the movie business so you might as well start practicing the new ethic, one element of which is people are Kleenex; you can take 'em, use 'em and throw 'em away, there are always available fresh ones. There is nothing whatsoever wrong in that attitude. That is the industry standard. You will be acting altogether properly in accordance with your new moral code since you will have achieved your objective: you will have gotten your movie made and received screen credit.

Will that make you a monster? Of course it will. Becoming a monster seems to be one of the great joys of the business. You can become more and more of a monster as you achieve further successes.

And by the way, don't worry about paying your original investors back. Stanley Kubrick didn't.

33

PLAN F:
THE INDEPENDENT
PRODUCER

Plan F is the end of the line.

F for almost failure.

Take your project to an independent producer.

Once upon a time, there were a few low budget independent producers, Roger Corman being the best known and most successful, who would finance and distribute the first efforts by young screenwriters, and even let them direct sometimes. A number of major talents got their first breaks from Roger and, for many years, he could get his good films into significant theatrical distribution. Nowadays, however, theatrical distribution is just too difficult, and even Roger is producing primarily for cable television.

There are still active independents today, but brother, is that ever a tough way to go.

You may get paid less than WGA minimum and maybe a great deal less than minimum. Your producer will tell you he has all the production funds but he will almost immediately change his mind and try to raise the money from others, and you won't be sure he has enough until the finish of post-production.

The budget will be lean, verging on inadequate. You can expect to be rewritten by other writers you never hear about and others on the project, actors, assistant directors, the cameraman, the go-fers. You may hate the finished project.

You will very likely discover that your independent producer is primarily interested in making deals, not your movie, and has obtained his financing by presales of various territories and various other markets, dampening the financial returns in the unlikely event it is a successful picture, and that theatrical distribution is a near impossibility. Your independent producer will screen the movie once or twice to distributors and dump it quickly onto cassette and cable if the distributors are, as usual, rudely unenthusiastic.

Doesn't an independently produced picture ever make it? Yes, of course. You may get a BILLY JACK or a GREEK WEDDING.

Correction: you can't count GREEK WEDDING as the success of an independent. Tom Hanks sponsored GREEK WEDDING. Tom Hanks is Plan A, since no green-lighter can say no to him, Plan B, the star of all star elements, Plan C if his agent was involved, Plan D, producer and Plan E, instrumental in raising the money. No studio marketing department to whom the picture was offered by Hanks could possibly refuse the distribution.

Yet, every once in a great while, maybe even twice in five years, a successful independently produced picture does come along and who knows, if you are lucky, it could be yours.

Hope springs eternal, even in L.A., and dreams are appropriately the fire that fuels the dream business.

Do keep at it. Success could be yours. Like the little engine that could, you can, you can.

You can sell your screenplay and get your movie made.

You, too, can make it in the movie non-business.

Good luck, keep the faith, and the passion.